Fallen Angel

Fallen Angel

✦

The true story of One family's Undying Effort to save their son from a life of addiction and of homelessness

Lucinda Esperanza

iUniverse, Inc.

New York Bloomington Shanghai

Fallen Angel
The true story of One family's Undying Effort to save their son from a life of addiction and of homelessness

iUniverse books may be ordered through booksellers or by contacting:

iUniverse
1663 Liberty Drive
Bloomington, IN 47403
www.iuniverse.com
1-800-Authors (1-800-288-4677)

Because of the dynamic nature of the Internet, any Web addresses or links contained in this book may have changed since publication and may no longer be valid.

The views expressed in this work are solely those of the author and do not necessarily reflect the views of the publisher, and the publisher hereby disclaims any responsibility for them.

ISBN: 978-0-595-48862-9 (pbk)
ISBN: 978-0-595-60874-4 (ebk)

Printed in the United States of America

Contents

Introduction

This is a true story of our 33 year struggle, fighting to save the life of our beloved son, Jason. During the course of that time, friends and acquaintances, who knew bits and pieces of our story, would often remark of our courage and say that they would have just written him off. I always said, "No, that is what would take the courage, we don't have that kind of courage." I have decided to write this book as a source of encouragement and hopefully, as an aide for parents currently experiencing what we experienced.

I, at first entitled this book "Street Addiction" because that is the term that so many parents in my Tough Love groups have used to describe their problem with their children. At the time that I was attending these groups, I had already realized that Jason's problem was a drug addiction not a "street addiction" which I knew was most likely the case with their child also. I know that this is a difficult realization and it is with only a true love and understanding that I have completed this book. I decided to change my title to *Fallen Angel* because our problems with Jason were many faceted, and this title more closely expressed how I really felt about our son.

It was our sincere effort to record these events as accurately and chronologically as possible. I have not used my real surname; in most other cases I have used first names only. My husband, our daughter and I conferred with each other and came to consensus that our memories were accurate and as chronological as possible. Up until now, I have resisted telling our story, because I did not want to relive the pain and also because I really hoped that the story was not complete and that the ending would be a happier one. It has been a difficult story to write because we have repressed many memories that were too difficult to deal with. Also, because these times were so action packed, and so terrifying that the sequence of events is difficult to put into proper order. Now that our son is in his mid 30's, it seems that our story is complete and somewhat bitter sweet. The ending is not what we had hoped for but it is much better than I expected. In retrospect, I would have done very little differently. I would have acted sooner, perhaps, but in most cases, not differently. In my summary I will expound on what I have learned in order to help and encourage others now experiencing the same struggles.

I would like to dedicate this book to my parents, Robert and Marcelle, who were very close to Jason as a child and a real support to me. I will always be grateful for the help they gave me. When I would just be totally worn down and frazzled by his hyperactive and oppositional behavior, I would call them and they would come and pick him up for a few days until I could regroup and present a more pleasant attitude toward him. They helped me maintain a logical response to his behavior, often calling for confrontation, while my husband fought me to maintain peace at <u>ANY</u> cost. He would respond to Jason's loud outbursts by asking me repeatedly the infuriating question, "what are you doing to him now!?"

I would also like to dedicate this book to our younger daughter, Brandi. Brandi saw herself as the "glue" that kept our family together and maintained an almost perfect child persona. She endured the unfair judgments from other families about our family based on their knowledge of our son's behavior. Some of her friend's parents forbade their children to associate with her. She endured preconceived attitudes from her teachers who had taught her brother earlier. Her defense to that was to walk into the classroom on the first day of school and announce, "Yes, I am Jason's sister, but I am NOTHING like him!" She, in her immaturity, would scream, cry and beg us to give him whatever he wanted just to keep him from running away, whenever there was a confrontation. Therefore, unwittingly, she became an object of his manipulation and a part of the problem. She endured, as did we, disparaging remarks said, just loud enough for us to hear, by strangers in public places. The subject being our son's multicolored spiked up Mohawk, studded leather "punk" wardrobe, or disrespectful attitude. I have often wondered why people were so hateful that they felt compelled to injure us further with the comments they made. There could have been no other reason for their comments but to hurt us. Did they think WE chose his look; did they think that was our WORST problem, did they not believe in "picking their battles?" Perhaps were they just insensitive souls with the good fortune of never having a child like Jason and therefore, lacked understanding.

As a college student, Brandi confided in me that she had such a wonderful childhood until Jason turned 13 and from then on her life was "hell". I said, "I was sorry that that had happened to her but that she would not be the wonderful person she is today had she not had that experience." She agreed that God had a plan for her life and that she was "in training." She went on to get her bachelor's degree in Psychology with a goal to become a family counselor, then went on to get her master's degree in special education and is now working in the San Diego School system. Her classroom is comprised of a group of emotionally disturbed students, a group that most teachers avoid but that she feels very comfortable with. She feels she was lead to this position through the lessons she learned grow-ing up. She loves her work, sees her students with loving and understanding eyes, and is very dedicated. The world is a better place because she is here.

Of course, all this did not all happen overnight. If it did, we would surely not survive it. At first he was just a difficult hyperactive, oppositional and stubborn child. That said, if I had to pick an age where it all really fell apart and swung beyond our control—I would have to say it was age 13 and with the beginning of drug use.

Until recently, I believed his drugs of choice were crystal methamphetamine and ecstasy. Both are amphetamines. My guess is that he first used them at a Rave club. He would usually "stage uproar" and run away so that he could attend these forbidden concerts. I know also that crystal methamphetamine is the drug of choice in the gay community. Both crystal meth and ecstasy extremely heightens sexual pleasure. He told me once that he didn't remember who he had sex with, that he was so out of his mind. Knowing Jason, I do think it was only with females, but I was concerned about AIDS and other STDs because of the casual, promiscuous and indiscriminate nature of this group of drug using kids.

Jason tends to be somewhat of a hypochondriac. During one of his brief returns home the local news stations were having the annual colorectal campaigns on TV. He said, "I have that! I need to get a test!" After listening to that for sev-eral minutes, I said, "You are not going to die of colorectal cancer, you are going to die of AIDS if somebody doesn't kill you first" The next day he went and got an AIDS test. It was negative but it marked the beginning of his long journey down a road of "self examination".

1

Pre-Natal Years

"We are all products of our environment." "We reap what we sow." Therefore, I must tell you a little about our childhoods and our families before I begin this story. This portion of our story is solely my perception and my interpretation of our families and should only be taken as such.

This is the story of our son Jason, Phil is his father. My name is Cindy and I am his mother. Our younger daughter's name is Brandi. Jason was not from a broken home. Phil and I have been married for 43 years. With the exception of disagreements about Jason's discipline, and only during his teenaged years we have lived a very peaceful and happy life. Both my parents and Phil's parents have been married for well over 65 years. They also live a peaceful life. Phil was the first born of his siblings. He was born during WWII, and then next to him is his sister, two years younger, and then 3 brothers. We are closest to his sister. Two of Phil's brothers have dropped out of the family as did Phil's father's twin. I am wondering if this withdrawal from family has its origin with some type of a genetic predisposition. No one seems to have a satisfactory explanation for it, just a comment that "he was always a loner".

Phil's family is deeply religious. They are Southern Baptists. Phil was never allowed to go to movies, to dance or to play cards. Of course, drinking or smoking was out of the question, as well as listening to most music. Phil was quite an athlete in high school. He played football, basketball, and track but his parent's never found time to attend a single game. He also worked on a farm near his house in Michigan. His parents moved to Washington the summer between Phil's junior and senior year of high school. The farmer he worked for asked his parents if Phil could stay on the farm and work and finish high school in Michigan. Phil was at the very top of his class. He owned and maintained his own car and had a trained hunting dog, which he had to leave behind when his parents refused to let him stay to work and live with the farmer and finish his senior year of high school. Phil still considers moving at that point in his life a tragic event.

He was not able to play in sports in Washington because he could not afford the insurance. Insurance was provided for athletes in Michigan. He got one "B" in his new school, ruining his straight "A" record. He missed his friends, his car, his dog and his job. He had to pay for his own books and tuition at the University of Washington plus pay his parents for his room and board. It was very hard to do by doing yard work.

I believe that Phil's father never really bonded with Phil because he was away in the war and never spent any time with him until Phil was about three years old. Phil's mother openly has her 'favorites' and is very vocal about expressing it. She is always very surprised when you respond to her comments with "Ouch, that's hurtful." I feel that Phil's mother did damage to her children in two ways. She always expressed how she "didn't feel right in fancy places," which to a Michigan farm girl was just about any place. She also would never say anything nice to her kids or about her kids for fear that they would get "the big head." She severely criticized Phil for being a University of Washington student and therefore having the "big head." While he was attending the university, and paying room and board he was also buying his own clothes. Once his clothes went into the laundry, he never saw them again, except on his brothers. I don't think Phil's parents thought it their responsibility to cloth their kids. His sister only had one skirt, one blouse and one cardigan sweater all through high school. The boys only had what Phil bought. Attending college was very difficult both emotionally and financially for Phil. He did receive a small scholarship but his father's high income precluded him from many at that point in time. Phil could not afford to live on campus and could not afford transportation. He had to find a daily ride to and from school, which he managed to do. Phil is an excellent swimmer and was asked by the swim coach to join the swim team. He had to say "no" due to his ride situation. He was also asked to join an academic fraternity which he had to turn down due to finances. Occasionally, Phil will become irrationally sensitive to joking and mild teasing and he will suddenly snap back. I think it is just a sudden memory of something in his past that makes him feel inadequate.

Phil's Dad always read his kids stories and Phil did the same for his kids and now for his grandkids. I think that must be one of Phil's fondest memories of his childhood along with fishing and hunting. It is and was so enjoyable for him to do with his kids and grandkids later in life. He was also very close to his maternal grandfather. He provided an excellent grandfather role model for Phil. Phil now really dotes on his grandkids. I believe that Phil often felt pressure from his strict and unyielding upbringing and did not want to duplicate that with our children. Unfortunately, he would inadvertently train Jason to throw fits to get his way, allow him self to be manipulated, and he would avoid confrontation. Confrontation was frequent and seriously dangerous in his own childhood.

I also was a first born, and every bit as independent and determined. I had a fiery personality and we were attracted to each other from the moment we met. We met on a blind date when Phil was a junior in the college of engineering and I was a senior in high school. Phil's parent's were panicked that he was dating a girl not from his church and they immediately started bringing home 'nice', more appropriate girls' for him. I joined their church but was still not considered worthy.

I was brought up to believe that I had absolutely no career restrictions due to my sex. Still my parent's held a definite double standard and demonstrated an extreme protectiveness in raising me. I often wondered when this very non-sexist attitude they talked about was scheduled to begin.

I have a brother that is 6 years younger than me and is a really wonderful, loving and hardworking person. He has one daughter. My father just exudes morality and fairness. My brother has an exact copy of this trait. Surprisingly, my brother was allowed almost total freedom growing up. When I would complain about the double standard I was simply told, "That's the girl's parent's problem." I know that sounds like a contradiction to the "morality" trait but I truly didn't believe that my parent's believed that for a second.

I have a sister that is three years younger than me and is a very angry, bitter person, who constantly insults me and needles me. Looking back to our childhoods, she was always antisocial except where it could benefit her in some way. She also loves to stir up trouble and see others unhappy. It is to the point of researching private information and saving it to use against people if the opportunity should ever arise. When at the University of Washington she managed to get a position in the office and gain access to student records. At a family gathering she spewed out this information on several people as a way to elevate herself by comparison and she was stupid enough to say how she got the information. I was shocked at the inappropriateness and breach of trust. I have doubted her integrity ever since. She can go from being perfectly charming to absolutely nasty and demanding in an instant. In our younger days I guessed that she had the worlds' worse case of PMS but she is way too old for that now and she is getting worse with age. She is a doctor of pediatrics and if there was ever a competition, she has beaten me many times over. She has no children. She constantly tries to create disharmony between me and our family. She lies when confronted and my parents believe her over me every time. My mother pretends not see her flaws but 'walks on eggs' not set her off. Her behavior and attacks are outrageous, mostly directed against me. She is extremely aggressive with a constant need for attention. This is not a diagnosis but she has many traits of a narcissistic personality.

I really wanted our children to get along, so I was very careful not to model an unloving relationship between me and my sister to them.

However, even as very small children they started asking me why Aunt Cheri was so "mean" to their mommy. My answer was always the same, "she just doesn't like herself very much so she needs for you to be sweet to her." That was also my standard answer for them when other children were "mean" to them.

Phil would get really upset about the way I handled my sister's abuse. He felt that I was not defending myself. I wanted him to stay out of it but his need to defend me was sometimes too much for him to control. My attitude was that:

A. It really did not bother me because she, by her behavior, has lost her importance to me. I could and I would ignore it, so as not to upset my parents.

B. She is doing an excellent job of showing the world what an "ass" she really is all by herself. She didn't need any help from me.

I just try to never to give her any ammunition and never let her push my buttons. I remain calm and unaffected by her abuse, a skill I perfected along the way while dealing with our son.

As you can see, we have some serious personality disorders in our gene pool perhaps even mental illness as in the case of my sister. I worry that Jason may have some of these narcissistic personality disorder traits.

At first my parents liked Phil because when I met him, I was dating Steve, a boy that they hated. He had just entered the military on a court order. They were very anxious to get me away from this 'unsavory character,' which I had dated for two years. Steve was always very good to me and quite the gentleman when he was with me. Apparently, he had some bad habits which I didn't know about, the rest I believe my mother made up. I believe they would lie to me even today about him if given the opportunity. Soon, when the former boy friend was safely out of the picture, Phil lost favor with them also. I was angry because I searched for a boyfriend that they would approve of. I thought Phil would be the one. Actually, they never liked anyone I dated seriously. At this point, Phil and I were engaged, I was 19 years old, and I was trying to make a good impression on his parents by joining and attending his church. My parents decided to add pressure to this relationship because after all, Phil was a "bum". (Translation: his family was of a lower socioeconomic level than our family was) My parents announced that they now would allow me so see Phil only once a week. That meant that we would have to choose to go to church, go on a date, or look for an apartment (the wedding was 3 months away). I decided that that was unacceptable and I left, temporarily staying at Phil's parent's house until I could move into an apartment we had found. Phil stayed at home and we did not live together until after we were married.

At the time of this writing that was 44 years ago and my mother is still angry and disappointed. She blames Phil's parents for the few weeks they took me in and she adamantly denies restricting us to seeing each other only once a week. They did not attend our wedding. Probably, because I did the unforgivable; I left home three months before our marriage. "Nice girls don't do that." I was not aware that our son knew this, but I believe this is why he was so adamant about attending his sister's wedding. My mother's attitude regarding Phil puts a hole in my heart and in our daughter's heart. It surprises me that my mother is willing to do that to Brandi when she was so injured by all the hateful things her own mother said about her own father all of her life. It is a real mistake to hate and to criticize half of a person's gene pool. It damages their self esteem. We learned that from observation. That is why we only see the good in our ex-son in-law and we would never say anything but positive about him and neither would Brandi, out of love for their children.

My big concern for my mother is that while being judgmental, she has an inability to put herself in someone else's place. For example she married at age 15, secretly. Now she brags that she was a virgin when she got married. I believe she is insinuating that no one else was. *Everyone* I know was a virgin at age 15. She doesn't seem to see the relationship between age and virginity. My response to that was that I wasn't sure that virginity was the most important hope I had for my daughter. I preferred that if it was between early marriage and virginity vs. education, she would choose education. Mother was shocked. She claims to have been really scared that one of her girls would get pregnant before marriage. Neither of us did. I don't know about my sister, but there was never any danger of that happening in my case. However, my brother got two women pregnant outside of marriage and his daughter got pregnant outside of marriage also. My mother believes that my brother and his daughter are perfect. Actually, I agree, they pretty much are perfect. What I don't understand is my mother's thinking nor why he and my niece are forgiven and I am not. I also don't understand why my mother can't see that Phil has been a good provider, we have a nice home and he has never abused me or the kids. He is not a drinker, a smoker, or a gambler. He is good with money, active in charity work, responsible, kind, and a loving husband and father. My mother's parents did not want her to get married either but she was only 15, I was 19, and still mom and dad were forgiven by their parents. Her reason is WWII was on, how about the cold war and Viet Nam, I know it was a police action but we all know it was really a *war*. I did not have our first baby until I had been married many years. We never asked for or received any help from anybody. From the day I left we were *totally* financially independent. I doubt that can be said of *any* of our siblings. My mother was under the mistaken belief that Phil's parents gave us the land that we built our house on. That is absolutely untrue. They did not even see the property for the first several years we owned it. She says that Phil's mother told her that. That is a lie on the part of one of them. It could be a false assumption on my mother's part. She is prone to those. It could be another fantasy on Phil's mother's part. She is prone to those. At one time, her fantasies made me really angry but now I think that she has lost touch with reality so much that she might even believe them herself. Phil will sometimes embellish a story or an event to the point that I no longer recognize it. It always embarrassed me, but I used to enable him by trying to cover for him. I no longer do that for fear that it will develop into his mother's problem.

The lack of parental love in Phil's life can't help but alter his self image. He wanted very badly to correct that by having a really great relationship with his own son. Jason's rejection of him was especially painful. Phil is such a good and loving person, he does not deserve that.

2

Birth

After 9 years of marriage and preparation, we were about to give birth to our first child. In retrospect, that long period of time we had together before starting our family, is probably responsible for allowing us to remain in the marriage through all these stressful years that you are about to read about. We knew that there was life before kids, and there would be life after kids. I am so grateful that we stayed together, although the road was rough.

The pregnancy was uneventful but difficult. I am just 5 feet tall and I gained about 75 pounds during the last half of the pregnancy. I worked as the Director of the Dental Assistants program in a private vocational college. The job could allow me to be very non-physical, but at this stage, just getting to work was getting increasingly difficult. I took leave the day before my due date. That night I had regular contractions and knew the time was near. By morning the regular contractions had stopped, never to return. Now, I had a constant cramp that got increasingly worse. My Grandmother was visiting me from Oklahoma, and I had planned to take her to lunch at the waterfront in Seattle. I had called my Doctor and told him of my symptoms. It was my exact due date. He told me that "NO one has their baby on their due date. "Its false labor, go ahead and take your Grandmother to lunch." I was not convinced so I stopped by the hospital on the way to Seattle. They kept me and called my husband at work. After watching my progress stall, they started a pitosin drip at about 11:00 AM. At about 5:00 PM the Dr. popped in, broke the amniotic sack, and proceeded to speed up the pitosin drip. Now, I am in agony. Several hours went by, of checking and rechecking and giving me more and more pitosin at a faster and faster rate, inducing no further progress but multiplying the intensity of my pain. The doctor again appeared at about 9:00 PM, eating peanuts and announced that he was watching "Around the World in 80 Days" in the Doctors lounge. "When the movie is over," he declares," if nothing further happens, we are going to do a C-section." He whirls around and returns to his movie. This is the first time he ever mentioned anything about a C-section. I felt a deep sadness. I was disappointed, scared and felt like a failure. My husband had to talk me into signing the consent form. I knew he would have signed it, had I refused. I never got anything for pain until I was actually in the delivery room and I am now dazed and exhausted by the constant pain. Getting the spinal block was a wonderful relief. It was difficult and painful to receive, due to my large size. I was unable to lean forward while sitting on the table so the medical personnel were really forcefully pushing me forward. Unfortunately the needle was pressing on a nerve that caused me to heave uncontrollably. At 11:05 PM Jason was delivered-a healthy 9 lb 9 oz. baby boy. As they lifted him from my belly, he just cleared his throat and his eyes scanned the room. He was beautiful! He appeared to be able to focus and he had the most amazed expression on his face. He was very alert, he never did cry. He was too busy looking around.

They immediately gave me a general anesthetic. I saw them injecting into my I.V. line and I objected but they ignored me. When I awoke in the recovery room, I awoke angry. I demanded to see my baby NOW! I was told that the babies were sleeping now. I ignored the response and I repeated my demand with yet more determination. I was wheeled past the nursery window and there was my precious little Jason lying on his stomach, head and shoulders lifted still looking around. He looked to be twice the size of the other babies and I believe he was twice as strong. I had never felt happier or more proud. Our daughter was several weeks old before she could support her own head.

The next day when they brought in the babies at feeding time, a loud smacking sound preceded Jason. He was searching wildly with his head and making strong sucking motions. We had to coax our daughter to nurse and continuously wake her up. From then on, I could always hear Jason Coming, as the nurses brought him to me. When the doctor visited me the next day, he told me that the cord was around the baby's neck twice so it was good thing that we did a C-section. I asked if, at any point he was deprived of oxygen. I was told "no, but I was concerned about the shape of his head. Clearly, with all those violent contractions, his head was being pounded into my unyielding pelvis over and over. I was in the hospital one week. After a couple of days my doctor came in to tell me that I had no milk. They weighed the baby before and after nursing and I produced no milk. This whole ordeal was not according to my plan and I began to cry. He looked at me and said, "What are you crying about? You are not a cow; cows are for milk not women."

After returning home from the hospital, I immediately fell into a deep post-partum depression. At the time, I thought it was physical rather than emotional. I was exhausted from the labor and surgery too. I would cry because I had to put some baby bottles in the dishwasher, that task was just too overwhelming. I did not recognize it as postpartum depression and when I complained to my doctor. He would just say "of course, you are tired, you are a new mother!" I tried to convince him that it was more than just being a new mother, but as you might have guessed, I received yet another flippant dismissal. Post partum depression was not a condition widely discussed in 1972.

3

Early Childhood

I took eight weeks off work and then placed Jason with a wonderful Dutch lady who took in foster babies with health problems. She simply loved them back to health. She was the mother of one of my students. Still I cried all the way to work, for days. The thought of leaving my precious Jason in daycare was just too much. My wonderful care giver cared for Jason for about two months and then she told me that she would have to give up Jason due to the foster care laws. She wasn't able to take in foster babies if she took in private care babies. I knew she couldn't be replaced so I gave notice at work and stayed home with Jason until he entered school. My days were structured with planned activities for Jason. Jason was a very demanding baby from birth. He wanted to be constantly held and fussed if I put him down. I believed, at the time, that you couldn't give a baby too much attention, so I held him constantly. Finally, I got a little carrier that held him to my chest and freed my arms so that I could cook and clean and go about my life and still hold him. This continued until Jason became mobile. I always excused this behavior with the belief that he was very curious and just wanted to see what was going on. Now, I feel that I unwittingly, taught him that the world revolves around him and that other people are on this earth to serve him. Jason loved to snuggle, he was playful and had a sense of humor. I bought a bicycle with a child carrier seat. We went on daily bicycle rides to visit a horse pasture near us and we brought apples for the horses. He loved to ride on the back of my bicycle; he loved the beach and the park and our walks. I regret it now that the Seattle duck and goose population has grown beyond a healthy level, but in my ignorance we also fed them. We lived on a man-made lake and that also provided a daily activity of walks around the lake. I also knew all the child stage plays in the area and other family events for children. We went to them all. He had such a cute and outgoing personality; it was my intention to get him into acting in these plays eventually. He was such a delight but so mischievous. I remember worrying about dying before he was grown and praying that I could just live until he was an adult. I didn't think anyone else could have the love and patience with him that I did. We joined a co-op pre-school to allow Jason to interact with other kids. I remember a parents meeting when some of the mothers were expressing how they were confused by feelings of anger toward their toddlers. I couldn't imagine feeling anger toward Jason. Everything he did was out of innocent curiosity or a childlike need.

We had a tiny little poodle for years before Jason's birth. The dog was not happy about our new addition and did everything to harass him. Jason had a little rubber Mickey Mouse that he loved. The dog would watch him play with it from a distance and wait until I left the room for a moment. Then the dog would run out and grab the toy away from the baby and run under the sofa with it trying in earnest to chew it up. On a rare occasion the dog would attack, growling and trying to bite but it was too small to get its mouth open wide enough to bite. It never left so much as a light scratch on Jason but it would teach Jason a healthy respect for animals and also an irrational fear of them. I had a pastel chalk portrait of the dog in the study for years and Jason would always remark about how much he hated that dog and how evil it looked. The dog died when Jason was about three and one half years old and he was still remarking about his dislike for the dog as a teenager. Perhaps this is why he doesn't like dogs today.

When Jason was about eighteen months old, I had just taken a cup of still boiling tea out of the microwave and set it next to the sofa. Jason playfully batted it, splashing the hot water onto his sleeper pajamas. Without saying a word, I immediately snatched him up and put him in the sink and started spraying him with cold water. I missed a spot under his arm and I noticed blisters there as I later removed his pajamas. I felt terrible. I put him in the car and took him to his pediatrician. As we waited in the examining room, I noticed that *Jason* was comforting *me*. His little arms were around my neck and his little hand was patting me gently. The burn was not nearly as serious as my damaged self-image of my parenting skills.

Jason was 18 months old when we took him to Disney Land for the first time. I had showed him pictures and talked to him about it for days before we left. When I went into his room to get him up the morning of our departure he was jumping up and down in his crib saying "happy, happy, happy!" Some people thought that it was a waste of time to explain everything to Jason at this age, but I have always felt that children understand language long before they speak it and Jason was speaking very well by his first birthday. I felt that Jason never had the separation anxiety that most toddlers have because when ever I would leave him with a baby sitter I would tell him where I had to go, who was going to watch him, they were going to read him stories and give him a snack. He was going to take a nap and when he woke up I would be back to get him. That put the time element into prospective and he always felt secure.

When our flight to California started to take off, I held him on my lap and had him watch out the window, pointing out the ground getting further and further away. It wasn't long until he jumped down on the floor and curled up into a ball, saying, "I don't like that what I see!" In a few minutes he was fine.

We met Phil's sister and her three girls at Disney Land and Jason had a wonderful time with his cousins. One of them is six months younger than Jason and has always been much taller than him. They developed a love/hate relationship that remains to this day. They haven't seen each other since their pre-teen years but this cousin still always asks about Jason. She has struggled with anorexia for years and has a form of arthritis. She has two healthy boys. The oldest of the three girls has a master's degree in international business and speaks three languages. She travels all over the world. She has no children at this point. The youngest is a recovering drug addict, is dyslexic, and has two boys; the youngest son is in chemotherapy for leukemia. She has left the boys in the care of their father. They are wonderful kids in spite of their tough life. Phil's sister is a sweet loving grandmother. She always makes herself available to her grandkids, which I am sure helps greatly.

I was really still recovering from Jason's birth when I was surprised by my pregnancy with our daughter two years later. I was very depressed by this pregnancy. Not because I didn't want another child, but because I didn't feel that I was physically capable of handling another rambunctious child and the ordeal of pregnancy and birth, at this time. Jason was the joy of my life, but what a handful! He was stubborn and willful. He was not diagnosed as oppositional/defiant, dyslexic or hyperactive, as of yet but would be later. He was also as quick as lightening and twice as impulsive. I always felt that he was a very bright boy, probably smarter than me. That is why I felt he was so difficult for me to raise. I would later find out that he did have a high IQ, but that he also was dyslexic, had hyperactive/attention deficit disorder and was oppositional defiant. This combination was a terrible combination for Jason. The schools did not deal with this well at that time. It really caused a great frustration in him and I think that deep down inside he was angry at us for not "fixing" it.

Jason did not accept punishment as a correction for wrong behavior. I would try to make the punishment fit the offence in a very calm and logical way. Still, He would be resentful and want to retaliate. For instance, if I took a toy away because he used it to hit something, he would be so angry he would go outside and gather sticks, mumbling that he was going to "tie Mommy up and hurt her." His sister, Brandi, on the other hand, would just "beat herself up" whenever she was corrected. She rarely needed punishment and usually just a talk would be sufficient. For hours after being reprimanded, she would say, "Why can't I be good like my friends they are so nice and I am so bad, I am a terrible girl!" Finally, I would say, "Brandi, its over, no one is perfect but it is my job to help you learn to be even better, I don't want you to beat yourself up you really don't deserve a beating." I only remember one thing that Brandi did growing up that was openly defiant but it was really kind of cute. She was still crawling and was so fascinated with the shiny bulbs on the Christmas tree especially when the lights would reflect in them. I was afraid she would grab them and they would break in her hand and cut her. We looked at them together and then I said, "Now don't touch". She looked right at me and slowly put her hand on a bulb. I lightly slapped her hand. She put that hand behind her back and used the other hand to do the same thing. I lightly slapped that hand. She sat down and took off one shoe and used her toes to touch it. I slapped that foot. She sat down and took off the other shoe and used her other toes to touch it. I slapped that foot. She then went around the Christmas tree blowing on the reflection like it was a candle. She continued that as long as the tree was up. That was the extent of her defiance. What a sweet little girl. As an adult she is not consumed with guilt. She is a very intelligent and kind, but a very assertive adult professional. I am very impressed with the way she always considers how every word spoken or action taken will affect her kids. Her ex-husband is the same way. They are both excellent parents. Our grandkids are very lucky kids in deed.

One time when Jason was under age three, he was playing quietly and suddenly he jumped up and poured water on the TV set, causing it to explode with arching bolts of electricity. I don't believe this was malicious just impulsive. At one time, he was playing with blocks on the floor while his father was sleeping on the couch. Suddenly Jason jumped up and gently placed the cardboard block container with a metal bottom over his father's head then turned and picked up two rectangular blocks which he used to bang on the metal end of the container. Jason laughed with delight as his father had what appeared to be a seizure and I came running, saying "No no, Jason, you will hurt daddy's ears".

We went through a serious biting phase where people were actually injured. It became so serious that we were asked not to bring him back to the church childcare. Finally, I had to set him down and explain that biting hurts and that he must understand that he is hurting other people when he bites. I told Jason that, "The next time you bite I will have to bite you to show you how it feels." I know

13

that a well known TV psychologist does not agree with me on that tactic, but you can't argue with success. The next time he bit somebody it was me. I repeated my explanation then I slowly bit down on his arm until he got a shocked look on his face and finally cried. I said, "See biting hurts." That is the last time he ever bit anybody.

Once while at a daycare, he picked the shyest child, lured her into a cupboard and locked her in it. He watched with joy, the panic as the childcare workers frantically looked for her. They finally heard her whimper and she was rescued. I was told that if any more incidents like this happen they will have to discontinue taking care of Jason. I think it was a power issue with Jason.

Our tiny poodle had died and we now had a part Collie and part German Shepard mix dog that stayed outside. We got the dog as a puppy and she loved and protected Jason. However, Jason never really bonded with the dog. He often filled the dog's water dish with dirt and pebbles. He would also wind yards and yards of dental floss around the dog. He didn't like dogs but he did not physically hurt animals. He seemed to really like cats. He had many fears and other people's dogs were one of them as well as any other large animal. He was also afraid of the dark and any medications. We thought this fear might keep him away from street drugs. Unfortunately, it did not. He was afraid of needles and roll-a-coasters, most Disney Land rides, and heights. He used to try to scare his sister by getting in the closet with her and telling her a big monster was coming down the hall to get them. As he would describe this monster to her he would eventually scare himself and go running and screaming out of his room while his sister sat there giggling. His fear of the dark and my insistence that he use a bathroom down the hall instead of the carpeted bathroom next to his room, would eventually lead to him urinating out his bedroom window. I started noticing a frequent puddle on his window sill and I thought the window was sweating. I would complain about it to Phil while I was wiping it up. Phil was also noticing a corner of the screen that was constantly pushed out of the frame. He would watch us and listen to us talk about this and chuckle but claim to know nothing about it. We had really big overhangs around our house so we had to have a really soaking rain to reach and rinse out his urinal. One summer day our daughter noticed a really awful smell in the front yard and called our attention to it. Upon investigating we figured out what was happening. By now he was a teenager and surely could have braved the short walk to his bathroom—after all, we did have electricity and lights in the house and on the pathway to his bathroom.

From age 3 through about age 5 he fought with his clothes. He would whine, twist and pull at them for extended periods of time. He would insist that I come into his room hundreds of times each night to fix his blankets, requiring that I move them up 1 inch then down 1 inch, then up 1 inch and so on. Whining and carrying on loudly until he worked himself into a full blown tantrum. I often would sit him on the porch in desperation so that he wouldn't wake up the baby.

As a 3 year old he locked himself in the bathroom for no apparent reason and began flushing everything in there down the toilet (I had to call the fire department on this one.) When I was in my 8ᵗʰ month of pregnancy with Jason's sister, he was playing outside the door and came to the door and asked for a drink of water. I said, "OK, Jason, I'll get it for you in a minute," a few seconds later he came back to the door again and said, "never mind, I drank the water like the doggies do". Panicked, I ask him to show me the water he drank, It was the puddle around the rose bushes, I was afraid of poisoning from the spray used on the rose bushes. I called poison control; they said to give him syrup of ipecac. Lots of liquids are necessary for it to work so I said," Jason, lets have a tea party" and took all kinds of cool aid into the back yard to tempt him. After pouring the syrup of ipecac down his throat there was no way he was going to drink any of my cool aid. I got out the garden hose and started playing with it and drinking water from it. Soon he wanted to play with it too. I took off his clothes, in anticipation of projectile vomiting, and let him drink and play to his hearts content. Suddenly he bolted and ran up the stairs and opened the gate without hesitation (he had never been able to open the gate by himself before). He ran out of the gate and down the middle of the street spraying projectile diareahha and vomit in his path. I ran after my naked boy yelling for him to stop. It took a full block for me to catch him. After all of this he had no ill affects what so ever.

From a very young age, Jason and I were in the habit of going on lots of walks and talking about and exploring nature. Well into one of these walks, when I was also about 8 months pregnant with his sister, he suddenly became afraid of pebbles and refused to allow his feet to touch the ground. I carried him all the way home. Jason has always had really odd, sudden and unexplainable fears.

One of Jason's favorite tricks in public places was to wait for me to become distracted and then hide and wait for the opportunity to lose me entirely. Often, he would hide under the clothes racks while I was shopping and watch my feet running all over trying to find him. He had an uncanny sense of direction at a very young age that allowed him to find his way around a huge department store by himself. Then, at the first opportunity, he would go up the escalator and go directly to the children's picture studio where I often had his portrait done, and say, "Well, my Mommy is 'yosted' again!!" "What is your Mommy's name?" they would ask. His version of Lucinda Kay was Cinda Loo Kay. I would hear "Cinda

… Cinda Loo Kay", over the loud speaker and I would know I was set up AGAIN. He spoke so well and so clearly in full sentences before his first birthday.

One day we were in a grocery store-Jason was about 1 ½ years old, I noticed a very large lady in a red house dress with big white circles printed on the fabric. The next thing I knew, Jason walked up to her and in a loud voice said, "Yeadee, you are so fat and you look just like a clown!" My heart broke in a thousand pieces for her. I apologized as I grabbed up Jason and immediately left the store. We went straight home. I said, "Jason, you should never say those things to anybody!" He said, "Well she **was** fat and she **did** look like a clown." I said, "She knows she is fat-she doesn't need you to tell her, she wouldn't be fat if she could help it and you hurt her feelings. That was mean!" I don't remember him saying anything like that to anyone ever again.

Jason refused to be toilet trained. I don't believe I ever did completely toilet train him. In retrospect, I think he retained his bowel movements until they got to big to pass and then he would get seepage around the blockage. His underwear was always stained and stiff with intermittently dribbled urine. I asked my pediatrician for help with the toilet training and other behavior issues and he would tell me to be consistent, make him do his own clean up, and use time outs. I couldn't have been more consistent; he would hide his soiled underwear, or take them off and throw them in the woods on our property. Now our granddaughter has the same problem and her pediatrician is much more knowledgeable and helpful than ours was. My pediatrician, however, did get me booked with a counselor in the Behavior science unit of Children's Hospital. She gave the toileting problem a name. He was inuretic and incapretic which was a control issue. The one thing he could control was what went in and what came out. The diagnosis was, we had a power struggle going. Actually, I already knew that and I tried to give him as many choices as possible but running amuck was not a viable option. She watched us play together, told me my parenting style was that of a teacher, told me that when Jason dribbled in his pants, he was "pissed off" and when he soiled his pants he was REALLY angry. That is a common thing for disturbed kids to do. She assumed that it was because we treated Jason differently than we treated Brandi. The only way that could be even a little bit true was in the sense that with Jason we were in a "damage control mode" all the time and we weren't with Brandi. Brandi got very little parenting due to our preoccupation with Jason. After working with us for a while she finally told me that Jason was the type of child that gets abused and that he was really lucky to have us as parents.

I really think that we were overly concerned about Jason feeling jealous when Brandi was born. When people would ask what they could bring for the new baby, I would ask that they bring a little toy for Jason instead. When People would say how adorable she was, I would say, "She is cute but not as cute as Jason". I would make it a point to leave the baby with Phil and take Jason to a movie and out to McDonalds and every time he would soil his pants in the movie theater. In exasperation I asked, "Why did you do that when we were having so much fun together, are you angry at me for some reason?" "Yes, he said, "I am angry at you because you had Brandi and I wanted to be the only one." "Are you angry at Dad too," I asked. Puzzled, he answered, "No, it's the ladies that have the babies." The only thing I could say was, "she is here to stay."

4

Grade School

I noticed that about this time, Jason began to enjoy long talks with me, about relationships with other kids and teachers. Later we talked a lot about girls and why they behave the way they do. We also talked about drugs, alcohol and smoking. We talked about strangers how you should never let anyone take you to another location. I taught my children to stand up for themselves and not to be intimidated by age or position of authority. I should have balanced that with a lesson in respect for authority for Jason. He mistakenly took it to mean 'RESIST all authority.' Brandi seemed to understand that you still needed to respect authority but not to the exclusion of protecting yourself. I had such of fear of my children being molested that my judgment may have been clouded. At that time, it was just coming to light that there is a lot of child abuse and molestation going on and the media was putting out frightening statistics.

Phil was an avid hiker and fisherman. He started taking Jason on hikes and teaching him about the woods, how to build fires and survive in the wilderness. Jason was having problems with his knees at this time and had many fears of the wilderness. He was afraid of bears, the noises in the woods and even camp robbers, brazen little birds that fly into your camp and take food right out of your hand. His hiking days were numbered. We lived on wooded acreage and Jason and his dad built many tree houses and forts in the woods. Our woods were full of kids and they had a wonderful safe time playing there and I loved having them all play there. When our kids no longer played there we removed all remnants of the tree houses. It drew so many kids that we were afraid that one of them would get hurt and no one would find them. We asked the local kids to stay off the property. It was too much of an attraction for them to comply so we removed all remnants of the play structures.

Jason was never interested in sports. He was unable to catch a ball. We tried to work with him on this but he had no interest. Organized sports were out of the question. The same holds true with my father, me, our daughter, and now my grandson. I believe it was and is a depth perception problem and that it is genetic. However, we all are excellent in individual sports such as snow skiing, water skiing, gymnastics, dancing, bicycling, and running. My father, Jason's maternal grandfather, made me some little water skis when I was a small child when water skiing was not a common sport. He later made trick skis. My father and I were really excellent water skiers. Dad started snow skiing at age 50 and taught all his grandchildren to snow ski, Jason being the first. Jason was an excellent snow skier. In jr. high school Jason turned out for cross country running and did great, but the program was discontinued due to lack of interest. That was very unfortunate. I believe that a sport often keeps kids out of trouble.

It was the disco days and it was a very exciting time. Phil and I took dance lessons, and started dancing. Soon we hired a coach, and worked out some of our own lifts and drops. We were so preoccupied and at odds with our child rearing problems that we really needed this time to reconnect and renew our relationship as a couple. We would look forward to our little break from reality, get all dressed up and go out to our favorite clubs. We would practice every night and the kids would get involved. Soon we started competing and taking the kids with us to Acapulco in the winter. Acapulco was a great winter get away. The winters in Washington are so dreary and Brandi and Jason loved our vacations there. Acapulco had the most wonderful discos in the world. We would stay in a really secure hotel where we could let the kids have some freedom and give them permission to charge food and drink to our room. We would talk to the hotel staff, tell them what they could have and then tip them really well. We felt that they were safe as long as they stayed within the hotel. I would let them take short trips together outside the hotel as long as they would stay on the main avenue, which was heavily guarded by armed police, stay together and come right back. Looking back on it, that seems like really risky behavior. I don't think I would do that today. I remember warning them that little blond blue-eyed kids are worth a lot of money in Mexico so be careful, follow my rules and come right back. I really had no idea of the extent of the dangers out there!

There was one disco that we really loved that would open every night with the theme from 2001 and a strobe light and laser show as the round light bar slowly and dramatically came down from the ceiling with strobe lights twirling. It had the effect of a space craft landing. It was wonderful! When Jason was 15 and joined us one week after we arrived we wanted him to see it. What we did not know was that on a previous night they had filmed us dancing. When the screens came down they replayed us dancing. Jason was mesmerized by the opening and was looking around in excited amazement when all of a sudden he noticed that the film was of us. He said, "Hey, that's you!! I am so embarrassed!" Some college aged kids overheard him and came up to him and said, "That is so cool, you should be proud of your parents!" That was enough to encourage him to stay for a while.

In about 3rd grade, Jason was out on the playground sympathizing with a friend during recess. The other boy's parents were going through a divorce. The 2 boys decided to run away together. Jason was really not having any problems at home at the time. I really don't know how running away could help his friend but never the less, they must have thought it would solve something. They left about midday and walked along a road which had been washed out by a severe rain and had a huge wide and deep crack in it. They managed to get past the crack and to a main road. After going an amazing 4 miles they stopped at a business along the way. The owner questioned them and called the police. By now the school had missed them. The police had set up a search team and a search headquarters. The phone call went right to the school and the police were sent to pick them up. The two boys had planned to make it to a large grocery store, another mile, and hide in the store until it closed and then eat the food in the store, gather supplies and move on. This really sounded like a "Jason" plan to me. Neither of the boys had coats on and it was fall, it got really cold in the evening and at night. I never really got an explanation that made sense about this incident.

In about 4th grade, Jason had a male teacher. Jason was the class clown so at first I thought this might be good for him. As it turned out, this man had no business in the teaching profession. At a parent/teacher's conference, this teacher told me that "Jason would never amount to anything". He really just had nothing good to say about him or his school performance. As I left, I suggested that he find another line of work-teaching was definitely NOT for him. It was about this time that Jason's behavior problems merged with his learning problems and the two problems could no longer be separated.

It also was about this time that Jason starting going to a little lake near our house and bringing back frog eggs to put in some little natural ponds that we had on our property. It wasn't long before frogs were jumping everywhere. I loved it because they helped with the mosquito population and the sound they made was wonderful. The only problem with his fascination with this lake was that he would come home every night covered with mud from head to toe. I would get so mad at him. I would spray him down with the hose outside before I would let him come into the garage and take off his clothes and then go into the mud room to take a shower. His best friends' parents finally told them that they couldn't play with Jason any more because they got so muddy. He would go through a pair of shoes a week. Canvas "Vans" were the only thing that would work out because they had to be washed daily. On Saturday I would take him down to the mall, throw his shoes and socks in the garbage and go into the store and buy new socks and new Vans. I thought that as the weather got colder the problem would go away but it did not.

Summer time is always a problem for working parents. There comes an age, about the summer between 4th and 5th grade, when kids are really too old for day care but too young to be left alone. I solved that problem by signing them up for one session of YMCA camp after another. It cost roughly twice what day care would cost but they were much happier with this arrangement. I never really felt that I could trust Jason to stay home alone all day. I had learned through my "Tough Love" group that summer time is often thee time when kids get into drugs and other mischief. The kids went to Orcas Island in the San Juan's and stayed all summer. Brandi got really home sick but made wonderful friends with the counselors. I think that Jason enjoyed it the most. They eventually got tired of it but by then they were old enough to have jobs or to be left alone. They had all kinds of fun activities and learned some really cute songs. They seemed to love it when an old Indian would come and tell Indian folklore and tall tales and cook salmon on a cedar plank.

After an entire summer in exile, it was really an experience going through their duffel bags. I never knew what treasures I would find in Jason's but at least there would be no dirty clothes. He came home wearing the same clothes he left in three months earlier. He never took a shower and he never took off his shoes which he wore in salt water, sand, forest and to bed. I put him in a tub of bubble bath with a cap full of Clorox and soaked him for an hour or so. The nasty black calluses he had on the bottom of his feet, sloughed off in one piece. Scary. I put his clothes and shoes in a plastic bag and threw them away.

Brandi showered regularly and changed her clothes but she put her wet swim suit back into her duffel bag. Everything mildewed. Her stuff stunk worse than Jason's and it really upset her that she smelled bad. She really couldn't under-stand it. It just didn't seem fair.

In fifth grade, Jason became a fan of Michael Jackson. No, he actually became Michael Jackson. He dressed like him, developed robotic movements and learned to moon walk in all directions. At school he did this exclusively. My little blond, blue-eyed boy even imagined that he looked like Michael Jackson. Well, maybe his skin color was at least as light. This boy, who could not read, could tell you how many pounds of equipment he used for his shows, how much it cost to do a show, how many people it took to put on a show and many other facts that he could only get through reading and retaining those facts. I worried that he could not just be himself. His obsession definitely pointed to an addictive personality and low self-esteem. This is the kind of person who, after beating an alcohol or other drug addiction, turns to other "non substance" addictions like religious fanaticism or food fads like becoming a vegan or vegetarian. True to form, Jason later became vegetarian. Now that he receives the positive strokes he needs from his career, he is still obsessive about his health but is no longer a vegetarian.

Brandi and Jason bickered constantly. From the day I brought Brandi home, I impressed upon Jason that he could never hit Brandi or hurt her in any way, no matter what. That rule seemed to take because they never came to actual physical blows. The bickering was non-stop and it drove me out of my mind. At the suggestion of a radio talk show psychologist, I decided to "pay the victim" as a solution. I bought a large sum of nickels and put them in my pocket. As soon as I heard an insult, I quietly handed a nickel to the victim. "Hey why does she get a nickel," Jason said. I replied, "Because you insulted her, she is a victim." I spent about 10 minutes doing this and about $1 worth of nickels, when I overheard Jason trying to work a deal with Brandi to take turns insulting each other. My own children were actually trying to extort money from me! I always felt that it was Jason who initiated the problems. He really couldn't leave Brandi alone for a second. She was younger but I felt more mature and she had much more self control. I wanted her to ignore him. That didn't happen. She also loved him and therefore was very vulnerable to his manipulation.

Brandi soon became part of the problem. He would get her screaming and crying by threatening to run away when ever there was a confrontation or things weren't going exactly his way. I could see the delight on his face when he was successful in this effort. About this time I became acutely aware of his lying. He learned early on that the best lie is hidden between two truths. Still, even today he could probably fool me with this tactic. For years, after they were both grown, every time Jason would talk to Brandi on the phone, He would always moan about mom and dad ruining all his teenage years by sending him to 'reform school.' He was trying to get her to sympathize with him against her parents. Finally, she starting responding with, "Bull! You forced them to do that with your behavior. You gave them no other choice!" After a while they stopped talking.

Jason was always "friend and defender of the underdog". However, he was always very mouthy and had a sense of justice which did make some enemies. I don't think Jason ever picked a fight at school, but I do think he finished a lot of them. He was not very sneaky. Often he was provoked by a sneak attack, which went unnoticed by those in authority. When he retaliated, it was *always* noticed. We were called to the principal's office numerous times to talk about Jason's 'fighting problem.' We had gotten the reputation of being the cooperative parents. We learned that a bully's parents are never cooperative. That was the problem. We were the easier route to the solution. In exasperation, we forbade him to fight. This was a terrible mistake; he soon became the target of bands of bullies and was picked on daily. It got so bad that he was afraid to go to school. We complained and complained to the principal and were told that the school could not be responsible for walking to and from school. I can see how bullies can just drive a kid to tragic action like the Columbine tragedy. They just don't let up and can really ruin a child's life. Jason's injuries were getting more and more serious; the parents of these bullies just wouldn't believe that their angel could be responsible for these unprovoked assaults.

We were now forced to take action. We explained to Jason that bullies are always cowards and they hangout in groups for that reason. We told Jason to wait for an opportunity to catch the ringleader by himself and just beat the 'holy heck' out of him. Tell him his buddies are going to get the same thing and then get them one by one. We promised to support him. A few days later I got a call at work from the school. "Jason has done something life threatening to another student and you must come and pick him up immediately he is being suspended". I asked what had happened and was told, "There was an incident on the playground where a group of boys were pushing and shoving Jason and Jason had ran away to another part of the playground. This scene repeated itself 2 or 3 times without incident. Then when recess was over, Jason waited behind the classroom door for the one of the boys (the ringleader), and swung his backpack around hitting him in the head. Inside the backpack was a very large rock and it split the boy's head open. The boy was taken to the hospital. It is the school policy to suspend Jason until further notice." I asked if all the other boys and their parents were called also. I was told that they did not have all the boys, as of yet. I said, "You call me back when you have them ALL. Then I will meet with the principal and the parents of ALL involved at that time." "Oh, it is our policy that when a child does something life threatening to another child they are suspended immediately!" An increasingly frustrated secretary told me. I replied, "Well it is MY policy to treat the problem, not a symptom of the problem, so you call me when you have all the boys and all of their parents." And I hung up. She then called my husband at work and got a similar response. Jason was never suspended and he never had another problem from these kids. The school never did call us for a meeting with the other kids and parents. Obviously this was still not going to be solved by going through proper channels. It is unfortunate that some people can only understand violence. I felt bad about solving the problem in that manner. I always tried to teach our son to solve his problems with his brain not his fists, and this was certainly contrary to that principle. I hoped that he understood that this was an exception to the rule.

In about 5th grade Jason's teeth became a real embarrassment for him. They appeared to be very large as all new permanent teeth do but his somewhat flared out. I knew that he needed orthodontics and I assumed that he wanted orthodontics. So I made an appointment and then I informed him of it. His response was, "no way, I'm not getting braces!" I said, "Oh, Jason I am so sorry I should never have made an appointment without checking with you first. If you don't want orthodontics you certainly don't have to have it. I will cancel the appointment right away." There was silence for awhile then he asked, "What will happen if I don't have orthodontics?" I responded with, "Well, your teeth will just get worse and worse and you will be kind of a funny looking adult and it might be hard to eat, but we will still love you just the same. It takes a lot of work to take care of orthodontics and your mouth gets pretty sore sometimes. You shouldn't have it if you really don't want it." "Well, I'll have it", he said.

It was when Jason was in 6th grade, that I received a phone bill that unrolled like a roll of paper towels. Jason had discovered the sex lines. 900 number after 900 numbers from all over the world, at all hours of day and night, except for school hours. Apparently, for a pre-pubescent boy this never gets boring. Of course, when questioned, Jason knew nothing about it. Brandi must have done it or one of his friends. I called the phone company and complained that I was offended that they were providing this smut to my child. They could make long-distance numbers not accessible from our phone but not just 900 numbers and they could remove the charges from this month's bill but not next month's bill. We felt that we needed long-distance service so we tried changing our phone number and not giving the new number the Jason. We called the school and gave them the new number but told them that Jason was not to have it. We gave it to Brandi but told her not to give it to anyone who would tell Jason. We knew that our secret phone number would not be secret for long but we were really just trying to make a statement about trust and responsibility. Actually he went for weeks, not knowing the number. Finally, someone called for Brandi and Jason answered the phone. "What number were you calling?" he asked. He then smugly announced to me that he had the number. "Well, finally," I said, "I would have had it within the hour!" We never had the "900 number" problem again. I understand that the phone companies can now just block 900 numbers only from your phone. If you have a child that might be tempted, you should just have them blocked NOW.

Next he went into the Ninja phase. This was a particularly worrisome phase because he would sneak around the neighborhood playing Ninja in a black hooded suit. He was now big enough to be mistaken for an adult. He looked like an adult prowler and I feared for his safety. He wore black Ninja suits and collected throwing stars; he read all kinds of printed material on the history and skills of a Ninja which he would spit out on demand. This boy was suppose to be very behind in reading and was to never go beyond a 4th grade reading level but he would read and remember a ton of facts and figures about subjects that interested him. At this time I was very naïve about what lethal weapons throwing stars were. However, Jason knew that they would all be immediately taken away *forever* if he ever used then against any living creature or threatened to use them in an unacceptable manner. He never did. However, at the time, I was extremely naïve about the dangers of these throwing stars and he would not have been allowed to collect them had I known that they were considered a lethal weapon.

5

Jr. High school

When Jason was 13 we were vacationing in Acapulco. Due to his school schedule Jason arrived one week after we did. When he arrived, I was very ill. As an example of how self centered he was at this age, he asked his father, "If mom dies will we have to go home, cause I just got here?" We could not believe it! He was serious.

During our stay there was a man that kept taking pictures of Jason. Jason would move away, thinking he was in the way of this man's kids, and the man would show up again, taking pictures of him. Jason came and told me about it and I watched him. He was right. The man was taking pictures of Jason and trying to talk to him. We had other similar incidents happen in foreign countries. I now think that it was because of my high level security clearance. These men were definitely under cover but after a while they always spoke to me. I think they noticed that I was aware and it was to put me at ease. During my security interview I was asked if there was anything that could cause me to divulge secrets. I said, "Of course, if my family was threatened, I would do whatever I felt I had to do to protect them". I felt that I and my family were watched closely in Mexico. I had to turn in a detailed report before leaving about our flight numbers and hotel and what we planned to do, who we planned to meet there. It never bothered me. I had nothing to hide. It made me feel very safe and protected. If I was wrong about this man, and instead he was a pedophile, Jason had already identified himself as not an easy target. He told his mother. I kept an eye on him but I relaxed a little.

While we were in Acapulco, there was a group of French people there who would strip off all their clothes on the beach to put their swim suits on. There was also a couple in the room next to ours that would stand out on their balcony naked. I wondered if they were nudists because of their immodesty or perhaps it was cultural thing and they just had no sensitivity for the Mexican's, more modest culture. We have always found the French to be very rude when in groups.

We warned Jason. The next morning we awoke to find him already gone. We panicked and started looking for him. We found him, down on the deserted beach, lying in the sand with his sun glasses on, just waiting for the show.

The restaurants in Acapulco, often give their customers complimentary before dinner or after dinner drinks, like a Baileys Irish Cream or raspberry or chocolate cream liquor. The legal drinking age in Mexico was either not established or not enforced, so we allowed Jason to drink it too. We also let him have an occasional beer. We wanted to take the mystery out of it. That was a bad mistake. Add alcohol to Jason and he turns into a monster. We told him that he should NEVER take even one drink. He did not have the ability or metabolism to handle alcohol and we felt that it would bring him nothing but misery. We forbade him to have even one more drop of alcohol.

When we returned home Jason got a job at Sahalee Golf and Country club as a caddie. He earned good money, was well liked by the golf pros, was often requested, and was often picked up and taken to big tournaments. Jason could be absolutely charming when he wanted to be. I often had school officials or parents say, "Oh, you are Jason's mother, Jason is such a nice young man!" It always caught me off guard because I had not seen this charm in him for years. I would say, "No I'm Jason Esperanza's mother." I soon realized that he knew how to act but that he chose not to at home. Jason studied all the books they gave him and became an "A" caddie in record time. The golf club had strict rules about the dress and appearance of their caddies. Jason was a very attractive young man and very vain about his appearance. He was now in his "Don Johnson phase". He dressed meticulously and fussed with his highlighted blond hair. The pros would often drive way out of their way to pick him up for a tournament and include him in their luncheon. One time he told me of a really elegant buffet lunch that was served at a tournament. He was absolutely starved when he started through the line. He knew he shouldn't eat in the line but there were some crackers at the beginning with some jam next to them. He thought he would just put some jam on a cracker and pop it into his mouth and no one would notice. It was the worse tasting jam he had ever tasted! It was really salty and foul tasting and he wanted to spit it out immediately but he knew he just had to swallow it and act cool. I said, "Congratulations, Jason, you have just experienced caviar!" Jason was getting pretty smug about his popularity and beginning to think that he was so sought after that he could make his own rules. One day he showed up for work with a bright blue Mohawk haircut under his caddie hat. When he took the hat off, he was calmly fired. I think this accelerated his downhill skid. Being fired both surprised and angered him. The fact that we predicted this when he came home with his new hair style made it even worse. This was about the point that he started experimenting with drugs. I believe he first used marijuana. With the marijuana came smoking cigarettes and drinking wine. I believe the use of cigarettes was a substitute for marijuana when he couldn't do that. It was a strong sign that I should have seen but I didn't. Jason's sister was telling me that Jason got high on the way to school every morning. His psychologist and the school district psychologist told me that we were lucky that Jason wasn't using drugs because this is the kind of child that gets into drugs. I chose to believe the professionals in spite of Brandi's persistence. I believe he used the wine simply because it was readily available. I bought it in big jugs and drank it every night. I thought that the taste would deter him. It did not. I discovered how I was making this easier for him one summer night when he asked me to set up the tent in the yard. He told me that he and a neighbor boy wanted sleep outside. We put up the tent and then later that night I awoke and decided to check on the boys. To my shock, the neighbor boy was no where around. There were 3 girls in the tent and my new jug of wine. A cigarette hole was burnt in the floor of the tent. Neither of us smoked, so I could do nothing about availability there, but I could certainly ban alcohol from my house. That was no problem since I was the only one who used alcohol of any kind.

I have a theory, that in order to dabble in addictive street drugs at all you first have to have an aspect to your personality, or some kind of personality flaw that allows you to put your immediate gratification above all those who love you. I say this because, we all know what the outcome of addictive drug use is and we know what it does to our families. Why would we risk bringing that kind of pain to those that love us if we had no selfishness in our hearts?

Jason is about 13 now. I would say that age 13-15 were his drug experimentation years. His attitude changed drastically and rapidly deteriorated further. He became very disrespectful and even hateful to us. His dress and hair style changed from neat and preppy pastels to darker colors and a wilder and less kept look. His sleep habits changed and he started to withdraw and spend more time in his room. The really nice kids that he grew up with quit coming around. His hair became more bizarre and more and more metal spikes started appearing on his now all black clothes. Ugly and offensive pictures and words started appearing on his raggedy black shirts. He started desecrating his room with offensive posters, cutting large tears in his mattress and his leather padded headboard, carving anarchy symbols in the woodwork and furniture. This went well with the horrible mess that he created in his room and the awful sounds of Punk music that so violently offended our ears. It was played at extremely high volume and I suspect it offended the whole town's ears. The language in these 'songs' was so offensive and so violent that it made me feel as though it was affecting his behavior. Something certainly was. I believe it started with marijuana, then he added some other drugs and within the next two years, designer drugs like ecstasy that he picked up at punk concerts. Surprisingly, he was a bit of a hypochondriac when it came to his health. Any mention of a disease and he was sure he had it. He was asking for a test for his new disease of the day when I said, "You are not going to die of that, you are going to die of AIDS if someone doesn't kill you first. Your life style is going to kill you!" At that point, he told me that he was so 'out of it' at concerts that he didn't know who he had sex with. At the time, I believed that the most dangerous drug he ever used was crystal meth, his drug of choice at that time. I learned later he eventually turned to heroin while living on the streets. Crystal Meth made him really violent and gave him super strength. It eventually led to my sending him away. I feared for our lives. I would find my kitchen knives in the shower, under his mattress in his dresser drawers and in all kinds of strange places. We had a Colt revolver that we kept unassembled with the parts hidden very well in separate locations. One day we came home to find it assembled, with a bullet half way in the chamber. Apparently we interrupted him and he left it as it was in our closet. He constantly rummaged through our closet. What he was searching for we never knew. However, none of the gun parts were hidden in our closet. We sold the gun the very next day.

The following winter brought this incident. We had had a heavy snow fall. The hill near our house had been sanded. The top of this hill is where the kids wait for the school bus. Jason decided to entertain his friends at the bus stop with the "amazing wall of fire stunt". He found a container into which he drained the gasoline out of the chainsaw and the weed eater. Then he walked to the school bus stop, poured the gasoline in a line crossing the road, and waited for a car to come down the hill. Just after the car crested the hilltop he struck a match and lit the gasoline sending a wall of fire up in front of the car. The terrified driver slammed on the brakes, skidding out of control in the middle of a crowd of kids. A very dangerous act in deed! Fortunately, no one was hurt but I soon got a call from the police department reporting the incident to me and asking me how hard I would allow them to lean on him. I told the police that he was just at the crossroads where he could go either way. I told them to really scare him and I gave them permission to use their own judgment. They waited until lunch time to arrest him, handcuff him, and take him out in front of the entire student body. Jason got a stern talking to, a warning, and was brought home and left in our custody. He continued pushing the envelope and instigating confrontation at home and at school.

6

First Love, Drug Use, and Fire Starting

Soon after entering Jr. High school, Jason started a relationship with a very beautiful girl. The relationship was very immature and unhealthy. Carry had emotional problems of her own and they were passionate about each other. She was self-destructive and often made cuts on her arms and experimented with drugs. They monitored each other's behavior and when one did something self-destructive the other one tried to top it in retaliation. Over dosing, and trying new drugs, became a popular choice of behavior. They were constantly checking to see if the other one "cared" enough. I became concerned about sexual activity and warned her mother that this might be happening. Carry's mother was in deep denial. Fortunately, no pregnancy ever occurred to my knowledge. This relationship was in full swing when Jason entered a treatment hospital. Whenever he would run away from the treatment hospital he would head straight for Carry's house, about 10 miles away. Carry had a very nice family but her Mother had emotional problems of her own. Surprisingly, she was a former psychiatric nurse. She was obviously stressed by her family situation. She was very nervous, talked to herself constantly, and she constantly scratched her face until it bled. Carry's younger sister was a friend of Brandi's and seemed very well adjusted. Her father designed marinas and was very kind, calm and friendly. Unfortunately, he was away working much of the time. Both Carry and Jason used and manipulated me and Carry's mother as well. Jason began carving and spray painting anarchy symbols on everything. At school they opened his locker and found it full of Volkswagen and Mercedes emblems. Apparently when I drove him to church so he could attend with his girl friend he stayed in the parking lot while she attended and stole the emblems off the cars belonging to the congregation. The emblems were then put on a string and sold as necklaces. The money was used to buy marijuana or other drugs, apparently. I had no idea that he wasn't attending church but I'll bet Carry's mother knew and wondered why I would drive Jason all the way there just to hang out in the parking lot. I wonder why she didn't tell me.

Jason also began starting fires in waste cans and around the outside of the house. Living in a 2 and a half acre cedar grove made this a big concern. He often threatened to burn our house down. I felt that the small fires he started were a way of intimidating us into believing that he would follow through on his threat. Now I felt that he was becoming a burden on society and there was a time, that I felt tremendous guilt for bringing him into the world and exposing society to such a menace.

One day I came home from work to find all of the water facets in the house sprayed water in an unusual manner. Jason had removed all of the screens in them to use to make bongs to sell for drug money. Jason's behavior was becoming more and more disrespectful and abusive at home. The "F" word became a major part of his vocabulary. No sentence was complete without at least three derivatives of the "F" word. That was a word that was not allowed to be uttered in my house. We learned through counseling to never let him push our buttons. When we lose control we give control to him. I still feel anger welling up inside of me when I overhear that word. I would immediately lead him to the porch, his new form of time-out.

His school work was really falling down and the district psychologist began working with us. She told us that we were so fortunate that he was not using drugs because it is kids like this that have drug problems. Our daughter said, "Hello, He gets high on the way to school every day!!" No one believed her. At about this time we, once again, started taking him to a private counselor on a weekly basis. This psychologist did offer us some practical advice on how to manage our 'out of control' son. I always found psychologists more helpful for us than Psychiatrists. They offered us practical advice. Psychiatrists never seemed to do that. We used counseling for Jason from age 3 to age 18. At this point the counseling was more of a help for us. It wasn't doing anything for Jason's behavior or academic performance but it was offering a life line to us, our sanity and our relationship. Brandi was also now getting some attention and a sounding board for her feelings. This counseling service also had great knowledge and advice on the Washington state juvenile justice code. They advised us that we had to get into the system to get any help. We did that by cooperating with the legal system and accepting the help of the Child Protective Services' in home counseling service. This service alone would turn out to be a life saver when we were accused of child abuse by Jason. I will go into this later.

7

Legal Troubles/Treatment Center

Jason started running away whenever things didn't go his way. He was 13 when he started a regular practice of running away and this increased every year. At first, he stayed with friends and as their parents wearied of his frequent visits, he found more creative places to stay, like sheds, and canopied boats, boat houses, in attics and houses under construction. At one point Jason and a friend, Ryan, broke into a house under construction and tried to start the furnace by lighting some poor work slips on fire and dropping them down the heat vent. They did not burn completely and there was Jason's name in black and white. It did burn the carpet and do some other damage to the construction however. It wasn't long until the police came calling, with partially burned poor work slips in hand. The contractor took Jason and Ryan to court and demanded that he be paid for the damage. I went to juvenile court with Jason as did his friend Ryan's mother. The difference was that I ask the judge to punish Jason to the fullest extent of the law and Ryan's mother lied for him. Ryan was released on the spot and Jason went to juvenile detention. I felt that Ryan owned more of the responsibility than Jason because Ryan's room contained unaccounted for microwaves, mini refrigerators and all kinds of extras that there was no explanation for. Jason told me that Ryan took over his parents' garage and fixed it up as his own private apartment. He would not allow his parents to enter. Once Jason witnessed his mother trying to enter and Ryan hit his mother in the face hard with his fist. Jason knew that there would be lots of questions to answer followed by an investigation on my part if things like this showed up unaccounted for in his room. This really made Jason bitter and he asked me why I didn't lie for him like Ryan's mother did. I said, "I don't care what happens to Ryan but I do care what happens to you. I want you to learn your lesson as a juvenile; I don't want you to end up in adult prison where it is really scary. Ryan's mother thinks this was easy but she has got a lot of tears ahead." The last thing I heard about Ryan was that he got a girl pregnant and got married. Shortly thereafter his name was in the paper. He was arrested for domestic violence. His parents are alcoholics in denial and I wouldn't be surprised if Ryan is now doing hard time as this book goes to press.

For this offence, Jason spent some time in juvenile detention. Then he was referred to Catholic Youth services to do community service and for a counselor to come to our house for some counseling sessions. This is exactly what I wanted. Now we are in the system. It is important to get into the system, if you are to get any help at all from law enforcement or government agencies. Up until this point the government only tied our hands and hampered us. They offered no help, only interference. This is what I refer to as "jumping through the hoops". You will read later how this particular 'hoop' really saved us". In an effort to prevent child abuse, children are told; if your parents abuse you call 911. They are not told what *constitutes* abuse. Abuse to some kids is having TV privileges taken way or being grounded.

Jason was now on runaway status more often than not and I was feeling like our home had a revolving door. At one point, I thought about putting a big "For Sale" sign with a 'sold' banner across it, cover all the furniture with sheets and check into a motel for a week or so. I thought that this might shock him into realizing that life goes on with or without him. I was tired of it. When he did finally come home I announced that we would no longer have the "revolving door policy". The next time he ran away *I* would decide when and *if* he could return. It wasn't long until I had the opportunity to put that into practice. He had run away and was gone for several days; I turned in a run away report, as usual. They always want to record of who his dentist is in case they find a skeleton. Other than that they don't want to know much because they aren't going to look for him any way. The police do not look for runaways; it was not against the law for a child to run away in Washington at that time. Parents were financially responsible for anything their child did whether on run away status or not but the child was free to be out there as long as he wanted. The judicial system was even talking about punishing the parent for their child's truancy or for the child breaking curfew. The thinking was that it would make the child feel so guilty when his parent went to jail that he would never perpetrate that offence again. That is a laugh. If a child crawls out their window, obviously the parent is trying to control them and enforce rules; otherwise he would walk right out the front door. If the child is out of control does he really have enough respect for the parent to feel guilt or is he totally controlled by drugs and devoid of empathy for his parents? Only if the child broke the law was he then returned to his parent. The real problem is that the child is never held accountable for his own actions, not by our legal system, not by the schools, and sometimes not even by his parents. Currently, I understand that juvenile law in Washington is much improved. The law allows a parent and child to go before a judge and set up standards of behavior, such as not running away, going to school every day, keeping up on a school contract and so forth. If the child fails to abide by these standards then he is in contempt of court and is punished by the legal system. I am so sorry that this was not available to us. It really would have helped and I would have done it early on, the earlier the better while he was still afraid of jail.

This time when Jason ran away, he apparently spray painted his school and was caught in the act. The police brought him home and I said, "Well, he can't stay here, I will hurt him if you leave him with me," "Do you have any friends or relatives he can stay with," the officers asked, "No, I responded, he has used them all up." They reluctantly took him to foster care. I knew that you had 48 hours of foster care free, before they start charging you. After that, they charge you 26% of your combined gross income and I presume that they take all your children at that point, I really don't know. They better at that cost; there would be nothing left to provide for the remaining kids. Since the law so effectively tied our hands I felt perfectly justified in using the foster care system to my advantage. They put Jason in foster care for 48 hours. Jason didn't have a room of his own, with his own TV, music, and phone, whatever he wanted to eat. He was watched constantly and surrounded by strangers. At the 47th hour, I called and said, "OK, I'm better now, you can bring Jason home." Jason was angry and bitter. He said, "That was really really awful," but it wouldn't be long until he arranged another confrontation followed by another runaway episode.

I don't remember what the blow up was about. It was most likely trivial and staged on Jason's part. What I do remember, is him backing me up against the wall, getting in my face and peppering me with hundreds of "F" words. I kept my 'cool,' although I really wanted to slap his face and push him away. His fists were clenched and I really thought he was going to hit me. In fact, Jason never actually hit me, intimidation was more his thing. Hitting was definitely against the rules. It was absolutely forbidden! There were other rules of equal importance that did not take root, however. I don't know why some rules were obeyed and some were not. My husband was standing by, ready to intervene if necessary. Suddenly, Jason grabbed a huge butcher knife from the knife block on the kitchen counter and came at me in a threatening manner. Phil immediately jumped between us and grabbed Jason by the shirt and the wrist of the hand holding the knife. He picked him up pushing him up on top of the counter to restrain him and took the knife away from him. Phil did not touch Jason in any other way. Our daughter was also witness to this. Apparently, Jason sustained a small red mark on his chest from Phil's reaction. Jason ran from the house not to be seen until the next day. It was still morning when CPS (Child Protective Service) first called me at work and informed me that I needed to appear immediately at their head quarters where a hearing would be held to discuss Jason's accusation of child abuse. I immediately called the Catholic Youth Services counselor who had been in our home and was on contract with CPS. CPS also called Phil at work and demanded his presence also. We all three arrived at the same time. The counselor spoke first, saying that "we do not have child abuse in this home, **we have parent abuse**." That single statement ended the hearing and prevented us from having an expensive trial and possibly temporarily loosing custody of our daughter. I think that this was Jason's way of running away but avoiding the foster care system this time. By getting his dad thrown in jail, to his immature way of thinking, he could then come home to overpower his mother and rule the house. The chain of events that lead up to our conference with CPS went like this; Jason went into the principal's office the next day and said, "My dad beat me up, showing him the little red mark on his chest. The principal followed the letter of the law and called CPS. CPS picked Jason up at school and proceeded from there. Our daughter's response was, "why did he say dad beat him up? You are the mean one, mom." I think it made more sense and sounded more dangerous to say his dad beat him up. It sounded funny to our family though, because I was the disciplinarian and used to get really angry at Phil for refusing to spank Jason when he was little. I felt that Jason was a kid that really needed an occasional spanking and he was too difficult for me to hang on to. Brandi said that she would never forgive Jason had he caused her to be put in foster care even just overnight.

Whenever Jason was on run away status, it was a good opportunity to get his room cleaned up. It would also have been an excellent opportunity to strip his room of all his belongings and store them. It was very distasteful to me to clean up such a horrible mess and I really did not think that anyone but Jason should have to do it. It made him really angry for me to rearrange his stuff. He would always scream at me for damaging his records which he kept laying all over the floor and walked over every day. That was so ridiculous that it did not even deserve a response. I looked at it as protecting my investment and an opportunity to check it out. Brandi always put on rubber gloves and helped me. It was very common to come across lines of powder that looked like drugs prepped for snorting. At first I would scoop them up and take them to the police station to have them analyzed, only to find that they were vitamin C or some other benign substance. After a couple of embarrassing incidents like that, I realized I was being set up and I started ignoring it. I never did actually find drugs in his room and I really took it apart when he left. I am still amazed by this. He was so disorganized, forgetful and sloppy that I didn't think he had the ability to hide it effectively. This is the reason that, though I was actually expecting a drug problem, I didn't recognize it for a long time. The only strange and possibly incriminating thing we ever found was a bunch of little pubic hair balls of varying color and texture. My guess is they were some kind of trophy collection. How bizarre!

The most effective punishment we ever found for Jason was to take his bedroom door off and store it under our bed. I will never forget the day he came home to find it gone and we told him he would have to earn it back. He immediately started wasting time by thinking of ways to retaliate rather than trying to earn it back. I fear that this oppositional personality trait will cause him many problems in his life. A well known TV psychologist advocates this now but also advocates taking away ALL their stuff with the exception of their mattress. The child then earns it back piece by piece. We thought of that but had no place to put all his belongings at the time. Now, that I realize how effective it is, I would be willing to rent a storage locker or rent a POD. It really irks me that I passed up the opportunity to get rid of those punk records for a while.

Stealing from his family became common place for Jason. He laughed at his sister for babysitting and then stole her hard earned money. Our wallets were never safe. Jason's soul was fading away and being replaced by a soul devoid of all morals. His entire being was goal oriented towards the drugs. He was now a Junkie. I no longer knew my son. He was not predictable because he degraded daily. He was becoming more and more violent. Violence was a new trait for him and a very frightening one. He promised that he was going to ruin us financially. He became paranoid. I would find my kitchen knives in the shower, between his mattress and box springs under his dresser, in the garage. He started cutting up his mattress and leather upholstered headboard and carving anarchy symbols into window sills and woodwork. At the time, I was working on a highly sensitive military program. I had a high level security clearance and we and our financial accounts were monitored carefully by security people. I am a highly patriotic person leading a squeaky clean life. I came home one day to find an American flag, desecrated, torn and with holes burnt into it, and an anarchy symbol painted on it, hanging on his wall. I refused to allow that in my house. It had to go. I felt angry every time I passed his room. I could not allow my home and my sanctuary to foster such feelings in me. I felt that my very livelihood was threatened. I decided at that point that I needed to decide whether to hide this from my co-workers and security or to be very open about it. I reasoned that I and my co-workers were not really a perfect group of people and that was OK. What was not

OK was if we were keeping a secret that would make us vulnerable to blackmail. It would have been impossible to explain the frequent phone calls that I got at work in our open row after row of desks, so I decided to be very open about my problems with our son. I kept no secrets. I shared it all with my co-workers. Oh, of course this was not always easy. There was the religious zealot that told me that Jason was possessed by the devil and offered an exorcism. He had incredibly poor timing. He would catch me with my adrenaline at a high level and would say things that would make me furious! There were the new parents that had no experience with this type of kid or any type of kid and were convinced that love could cure all. I wished they were right and I hoped that they never had to find out how very wrong they were. There were the ones that thought my husband should just "knock some sense into him". They had no experience with the court system and Child Protective Service and did not understand that just an **accusation** of child abuse could send us to court, costing us major dollars and worse, cause our daughter to be removed from our care. Most of my co-workers, however, were very understanding and supportive.

On Jason's 15th birthday, we had planned for his grandparent's to come over. They had made a real effort to buy him a special birthday gift that he had been wanting for a long time. He knew we were celebrating his birthday that evening and that his grandparents were coming over but he didn't come home from school that day at all. His grandparents were really hurt and I am sure felt really rejected. I told my mother to take his present back to the store. We did the same. He got no presents that year.

Holidays were usually a disaster too at this point in Jason's life. He had such a big family that loved him. We had had such wonderful family gatherings and traditions for the holidays throughout his life. Now he preferred to go off with his friends and get high rather than spend time with his family. It broke our hearts. Sometimes he didn't even bother to spark a confrontation to get away, he just left.

Jason often did things to complicate our lives for no apparent reason. Like the Saturday morning that I backed my car out of the garage to find a nail in each of my tires at approximately the same place. My husband went to work taking the tires off to take them down for repair with our other car, but before he backed his car out he checked around to see if there were any nails in the vicinity. He found a nail leaning and wedged into the curve of each of his four tires so that when he backed out it would surely puncture. This took up a whole Saturday repairing tires but it could have been worse had Phil not been so observant. We could have had 8 flat tires and no car to get them in for repair. I asked Jason what he hoped to accomplish by doing this. His response was "Why do you always have to blame me?! Brandi probably did it."

By now Jason was almost constantly out on runaway status. To get by and to get favors of food and shelter he would tell wild and dramatic tales of his tragic life at home. Surprisingly no one, to my knowledge, ever called Child Protective Services. Yet many people believed at least part of the stories he told. To me that is a shocking fact. Some felt so badly for Jason that they tried to intervene. One couple, in particular, took Jason in, talked to the school principal and then came to talk to us. They were very sweet and genuinely concerned. They offered advice and offered to take him in indefinitely. I could see that they had not met our *real* son at this point. We tried to tell them that, but they were so sure that he was just abused and misunderstood and that with a little love they could fix him. We thanked them for their concern, gave them one more word of warning and wished them luck. Two days later they informed the principal that they had given up and turned Jason out. They never bothered to tell us. Perhaps they were embarrassed, but they were still wrong. Years later, we heard that their daughter had become a stripper at a local strip club. No, judgments here, it's just not a career at the top of my list of career hopes for my daughter.

Jason's response to anything that we said to him became a really obnoxious sneer. Soon he was adding a hand jester that mimicked a masturbation motion. This would embarrass me terribly. I would get increasingly angrier and angrier at myself for being embarrassed over something that *should* embarrass him, not me. Then one night we were in a buffet restaurant—Brandi and Jason's favorite place to eat. Jason was ahead of me in line. When he got to the soup, he filled his bowl and then put his bare hand over the solids and poured the broth back into the pot. I was mortified! When we got back to our table, I said, "Jason, you just violated some very strict health laws with that move, we could get kicked out of this place and band from ever returning." He again embarrassed me in this very crowded establishment, with his little sneer and hand jester response. This time, I responded loudly to my husband, "Oh, look dear, I think Jason is trying to tell us something, He doesn't have the words for it yet, but I believe he is trying to tell us he has learned to *masturbate*! Isn't that wonderful, I am so proud, and how very *interesting* that he would choose to share that with us." Our daughter grinned played right along, She said, "Cool, I am going to tell all my friends on the school bus tomorrow." (I was surprised she even knew the meaning of the word) I never saw that dreaded hand jester again.

Shortly before that incident we had found our wonderful counseling practice that specialized in families with youths out of control. It was great because they assigned a specific counselor to us, whom we met with on a weekly basis; they also had staff meetings where they presented their cases in a roundtable discussion. We were offered practical advice which was very helpful. Our councilor shared this buffet restraunt incident in the roundtable and all the other counselors thought it was great! Academic testing was also done here, Jason was referred to Children's' hospital for neurological testing and a complete work-up was done. I can't believe that he was actually a teenager before neurological testing was done, after all my desperate attempts to enlist professionals to help me with this problem. In retrospect, I should have insisted on all of this when he was in early grade school. I did not know these things existed. At the time, I only knew that something was not right. My only source of direction was from my pediatrician. It was only a matter of time until our counselor had Jason admitted to a local treatment hospital. Jason was definitely out of control, not mentally ill but defiant and self destructive. The term "incorrigible" was stricken from the legal books in the state of Washington, at the same time that running away was decriminalized. The day he was admitted, we picked him up at school and said we were going to get something to eat. We were nervous because we knew that the state law required that Jason admit himself into this hospital of his own accord. He was over the magic age of 12 and it was almost impossible to get a court ordered committal now. To get a committal in the state of Washington you have to attempt a murder or suicide. "You have to be a danger to yourself or others." Prostitution, being a child living on the street or doing dangerous drugs does not qualify. A very determined, and as I later came to believe, a rather shady psychiatrist was going to be there to manipulate Jason into agreeing to be admitted I was grateful for him at the time, because I knew it would take some manipulation to get him to sign himself in. All of the professionals concerned in Jason's care, still believed that he was not using drugs. He was so disorganized I didn't think he had the ability to physically hide it and we were only slightly naïve about drugs—we were actually looking for them and seeing no hard evidence other than his behavior. When Jason realized that the plan was for him to stay there, he physically attacked his father. At that point we left him alone with the doctor. The doctor talked to him for about 20 minutes then came out and told us he was admitted. I am not sure, but I believe he was given an injection to calm him. Jason imagined this treatment center to be like the asylum in the movie, *One Flew Over the Cuckoo's Nest*. He was in great fear of any medication that they tried to give him. He suspected that a lobotomy was the next treatment that awaited him. It was a very depressing place and I would have preferred not to have him there. I sensed his fear and it made me very sad. At the same time I was grateful to have a safe place for him to be, getting more education, treatment, and our home was now a safe place for our daughter. Our own school district had a teacher that came to the treatment center and conducted daily classes. I find the committal laws for juveniles like Jason to be in grave error. How can you expect an oppositional/defiant child to willfully sign themselves into a treatment program. They are actually enjoying the behavior they are exhibiting. It makes them feel powerful. They don't realize the dangerous path they are on, they are to immature to predict the impact that their behavior will have on their the future, so why would they want treatment?

The treatment center gave us a list of clothes to provide and a list of what is not allowed. We provided all that was on the list and they all disappeared in a few days. I think that he may have cut them up and flushed them down the toilet. About the time he suddenly had no clothes, we came to visit him and all the toilets in his ward were plugged up. The treatment center complained that he was staying in his hospital pajamas all day. This was not a good situation to have around hormone crazed teenagers. I again provided the clothes and they again promptly disappeared. I was notified again. Now I had no doubt that he was destroying, throwing away, or giving away his clothes. At this time he was still promising to destroy us financially and actually, he was doing a pretty good job of it. I went the Salvation Army and picked out a selection of the ugliest polyester plaid bell bottoms I could find with clashing printed golf shirts. I put his name boldly in laundry marker on each item, placed them in a bag and took them to the head nurse. I said, "These are the clothes that I am providing *once again* for Jason. Please be sure that he gets dressed in them every day." She looked in the bag and started laughing, "I certainly will," she said. It became his "cool" trademark but I never had to replace them. This time at the hospital was a really difficult time. We had to close all doors for him so that he had no other place to go. We had to call parents of his friends and tell them what we were doing and that it was very important that they did not take him in. Many parents that didn't know us were just sure that we were doing something very wrong and felt that they could handle it much better. They offered to counsel us. We had to tell these well meaning but misguided people that we would have to bring charges against them if they took Jason in. We stressed that it was important to close all doors open to him so that he had no other place to go *except* the treatment center. We tried to relieve their concern for Jason by informing them that our entire family was receiving lots of counseling and that he was attending school.

Jason learned additional manipulative ploys from the other kids in counseling sessions. He once told me that he hated that treatment center so much that he felt like committing suicide. He threatened me that boys are usually successful the first time they try. I know that a suicide threat is usually a cry for help and should never be taken lightly so I did later run it by our counselor but my immediate response was to say, "There is really nothing I can do about it if you are determined to do that but remember that *suicide is a permanent solution for a temporary problem.* When I spoke to our counselor about it he told me that Jason was too narcissistic to commit suicide.

We had regular parents' meetings and meetings with his psychiatrist. I came to think of his psychiatrist as shady because he earned the bulk of his income as a professional trial witness in child sexual abuse cases. Jason knew that there was an incident that involved him and one of Phil's brothers, and Phil's parents that occurred when Jason was a toddler. It was an incident that really made Phil and I angry and caused us not to trust his parents with our kids and not to even speak to the brother to this day. Jason did not recall or know what had happened, but he knew something had happened and he knew who was involved. The psychiatrist convinced Jason that his Uncle had sexually abused him. This was presented to me in a counseling session as a big breakthrough and revelation I was stunned that they dug up this and I knew that this was twisted by the Doctor. I stated that "I hate this particular brother, that he is a lazy, spoiled, manipulative, religious fanatic whom I believe is capable of any evil—but the fact is that this just did *not* happen." Then I turned to Jason and I explained to him, that it was a simple childish incident, where his Uncle saw an opportunity, when I was distracted, to remove him from the room and take his jealousy for Phil out on Jason, by spanking him and then threatening him not to tell me. It was the intimidation that Jason felt that made me the angriest. I was there and could handle any discipline that Jason required. As it turned out, the only wrong behavior that occurred was done *to* Jason not *by* Jason. Apparently Jason had an alleged altercation over a toy with one of his cousins, by a different brother. The alleged victim did not even remember the incident 5 min. later. I did not see Jason being taken to another room. I did see him come out crying and he refused to tell me why. I took him to the car and demanded to know why he was crying. Finally, he told me that Uncle Mark spanked him. I pulled down his pants and his little bottom was just glowing red. I was so angry that I could not speak to Mark. Phil called Mark on the phone and asked if he had spanked Jason. Mark admitted that he did and said it was not the first time. Phil then asked the Mark very calmly, to, "in the future leave the disciplining of our children to us." This caused Mark to go into a religious tirade and tell Phil that we both "think we are better than everybody else and we are both going to hell!" Next Phil's dad got on the phone and Phil repeated his request. Another tirade occurred only with even more rage. Throwing up a totally unrelated smoke screen is a frequent defensive tactic in this family. If it were not so sad and ridiculous it would be funny in its absurdity. I never left my kids there again and only stayed a very short time with them right by my side after that. I never forbade them to visit their grandparents *with* their father or I, but I never forced them to go either. I really did not expect an apology. What I did expect was a reassurance that, "if that is the way we felt, they would respect our feelings." I never got that. After explaining all this, the doctor continued to insist that it still could have been sexual abuse. He would not give up! He was very persistent but so was I. I have always felt that encouraging a child to falsely claim sexual abuse was almost as damaging as sexual abuse itself. I was not going to allow it! For this reason, I called the doctor "shady." I really think he was just trying to drum up another sexual abuse court room gig and didn't care about the damage he would leave in his wake.

When the children were little, I would get angry at Phil for not spanking Jason when all else failed. Looking back on it, he really couldn't. It brought back too many memories of his "abuse." To clarify this, his "abuse" was mild and was somewhat acceptable at that time. A "spare the rod and spoil the child" mentality was common then. There are some that would say that we should have used the same parenting methods. However, Phil was aware that it did not make him feel the way he wanted our children to feel and he was determined not to do that to them. Those were feelings that he just could not allow to exist. We both agreed that we would 'correct' the mistakes we perceived our parents to have made. In some ways that was a good choice and in other ways it was *disaster*. We made perhaps worse mistakes of our own. I was determined not to try to make decisions for my children that were theirs only to make in their life choices. I always welcomed the mates they chose and treated them like my own children. I tried to always communicate with *words* to my children, not frowns, the silent treatment and innuendoes. If I had something to say, I said it. I didn't make them 'guess' why I was angry or even *if* I was angry. Phil was determined to always make each of his children feel safe, loved and special. He tried never to explode in anger. He has a very mellow disposition but the occasional blow up did happen suddenly and unexpectedly. His paternal grandfather was an alcoholic. I believe that is where this comes from. Obviously, Phil's father has this trait also and to a much more extreme level.

There is not a doubt in my mind that every parent does their best in parenting with the tools they have. I hold blameless any shortcomings in parenting that we were subject to. I hope my children do likewise for me.

The treatment hospital had two units for kids. Jason was first assigned with other out-of-control teenagers to the open unit. These were kids that were not a danger to the community. Secondly, they had the locked unit where they housed the dangerous, criminally insane minors. I can't recall exactly how much it cost, many many charges were itemized, and I would guess an average of about $400 to $600 per day plus another $200 for counseling sessions, and medical treatment. They would let the total get up to about $60,000 and then bill our insurance. Jason would often run away just before it was submitted. After 48 hours he would be automatically be put on "unauthorized leave" status. When he would leave without his doctors dismissal, the insurance would refuse to pay the balance and we would owe whatever the total was. It was really scary when he would run wild out there. He was panicked and wild eyed and he frightened people. I was afraid for his safety. He would often return and try to free all the other patients to create mayhem. Phil was really good at tracking him down and talking him in to signing himself back in. Finally, they put him in the locked unit and he even escaped from there on more than one occasion. That is a really frightening situation. There were some really scary people in this unit; one in particular, was a huge, 15 year old rapist. He raped all species, both sexes. Evil just emanated from him. Hopefully, he will never see the light of day.

Jason had a habit of getting angry and calling the male psychiatric nurses unflattering names regarding their sexual orientation. Often it was a good guess but very rude and immaterial. Not long afterwards, Jason would get a change in roommate assignments and find himself rooming with a homosexual. After a while, it seemed that he was *always* roomed with a homosexual, which made Jason very uncomfortable. Other than that, it was not a problem. Then one day he was roomed with the evil 15 year old rapist, who prior to this had been roomed all by himself. Jason was very intimidated by this boy, as was I. The way he looked at me sent shivers up my spine. Jason said that he would wake up in the night to find him standing over him looking down and smiling. Jason had finally had enough. He took his blanket and pillow and went into a multipurpose room and slept on the sofa. He was told that he couldn't do that and to go back to his room. Jason refused. He lost several points for that and told me about it the next day. I called his psychiatrist and ask if the patients at the treatment center are predominately homosexual. He told me "no" and asked why I ask. I told him that Jason is always roomed with a homosexual and explained the incident that happened the night before. I reminded Jason's doctor that Jason was not there to change his sexual orientation. Jason was again reassigned a roommate and the lost points were restored. I really hated for him to be in the locked unit. He was there just because he ran away constantly but it was a really depressing place. I still question whether putting him in this treatment facility was the right thing to do. At the time, our primary interest was to create a safe environment for our daughter and our selves and to allow him more school credits. The decision accomplished that. If faced with the same situation today, I would still do it for those reasons, but I would like it even less. I don't think the counseling at the treatment center helped at all. It just taught him to play the game more skillfully. Today, Jason is very much a gay rights advocate. In fact, he once intervened in a gay bashing and did some jail time for it. The gay bashers *should* have been the ones arrested but they were neat and tidy "jocks" and Jason was obviously in his street person grunge uniform.

Jason was once accused of assisting in an attempted rape while at the treatment center. I did not believe that he was capable of rape and immediately called his counselor. He agreed that Jason would never participate in a rape. Jason loved and respected women. Our counselor looked into it and found that there was another patient named Jason at the hospital. It was assumed that it was our Jason because the other Jason had no arms. Upon further investigation it was discovered that the Jason with no arms merely acted as a look out and our Jason was not even present.

Jason started playing the 'psycho game'; earning his points, by saying all the right things. He had earned an outing. I picked up his girl friend and took them to a movie. I now believe that his girlfriend slipped him some drugs during the movie. He came out of the movie with a different attitude. He wanted me to take him to buy some new jeans in a certain small store. While he was in the dressing room trying them on, he managed to slip out of the store. I jumped in my car and found him running down a road through a construction area. I stopped and begged him to get into my car. Instead he picked up a huge rock and tried to throw it through my windshield. I just sat there waiting for the impact and thinking, "go ahead, you have already killed me, let's just make it official." Suddenly he heard sirens. He dropped the rock on my hood and ran, leaving a huge deep dent in the hood of the car.

Again, crystal methamphetamine, made Jason frightfully strong and very violent. He once picked me up and threw me across the room, breaking my glasses, even though; I outweighed him at the time. Jason was a very non-violent person by nature. He had not seen or experienced much violence in his life and we did not encourage violence as a solution. He was taught that violence is rarely a solution for your problems. Smart people use their brains not their fists. He was also taught that people that use fowl language are just showing their lack of education and poor vocabulary. His language became horrible and he showed no shyness about using fowl language in our presence. His behavior was shocking and very sad for us.

Crystal meth creates powerful euphoric feelings often lasting 8 hours or more. The most popular method of using it is to smoke it. It can also be snorted, taken orally or injected. I believe Jason snorted it or smoked it. crystal meth is a form of amphetamine, or speed. crystal methamphetamine's chemical structure is very similar to amphetamine, but has a much more pronounced effect on the user's central nervous system. crystal meth is extremely addictive and using crystal meth causes severe, often irreversible, physical and psychological damage. It is a real problem here in Arizona because of our close proximity to Mexico, a big producer of the drug. It is linked to identity theft which is a real problem here also. The "cooking" of meth is very dangerous because of its explosive nature and the dangerous toxins it produces in the cooking process, getting into the walls and flooring of the building making it dangerous to even go into these places to arrest the perpetrators. Crystal meth has many street names including crank, ice, meth, tweak, speed, glass and chalk.

The symptoms of crystal meth use are: paranoia, anxiety, aggressiveness, hostility, tremors, skin abscesses, hallucinations, brain damage, insomnia, decreased appetite, sweating, euphoria followed by depression. Chronic abuse can lead to psychotic behavior including intense paranoia, visual and auditory hallucinations and out of control rages. Chronic users develop sores on their bodies from scratching imaginary bugs crawling on or under the skin. I have observed rages for no reason in Jason. I don't know if he was hallucinating but he was certainly paranoid and extremely aggressive and hostile. Meth use can also cause severe gum damage and their related dental problems, known as "meth mouth". Jason has very good teeth and has managed to survive being homeless without loosing his teeth. He currently is having a dental problem with his two lower front teeth. He has lost a major amount of gum and bone support, they are very loose and he is fighting to save them. His dentist is really baffled by this. I asked Jason if he told his dentist that he was a former drug user. Jason was shocked that I would consider that. The answer was "no". I think that information would clearly explain the situation to his dentist. Fortunately, I learned recently that he only used meth for a very short time and did not continue it after he left home.

Methamphetamine is a Schedule II stimulant, which means it has a very high potential for abuse. Addiction happens very rapidly. In order to get treatment, it is necessary to detoxify first because having the drug in your body just creates an urge to have more. The ideal way to detoxify is under constant medical supervision in a residential treatment program due to medical issues during withdrawal. Meth is the hardest addiction to treat. Meth addicts get over the acute effects of withdrawal fairly quickly, but the "wall" period, a period where the urge for the drug continues, lasts six to eight months for casual users and two to three years for regular users. I truly admire Jason because I think he kicked all his addictions without a formalized treatment program with shear courage and determination. Like I said before, he is the most stubborn person I ever met. Very few people are successful kicking it this way and if given an alternative I would take the alternative.

Like all amphetamines, crystal meth causes large amounts of dopamine to be released in the brain. Dopamine is a chemical that improves mood, increases self-confidence and strength and heightens sex drive. Unlike other amphetamines, crystal meth works mainly on the brain, causing fewer side effects on other parts of the body. The problem with frequent use is that people built up a tolerance and need larger amounts to get high. At higher doses, side effects on other parts of the body become more obvious. At very high doses people can develop brain-damaging fevers, stroke-producing high blood pressure, heart attacks and massive damage to muscle tissue that can lead to kidney failure and death. Long-term use changes the chemical balance of the brain and can cause a mental illness called psychosis. In the psychotic state, hallucinations are common. People may believe they are infested with parasites, which they see crawling on their skin. They come into the doctor's office with sores from picking and scratching at these imaginary parasites. If the drug is not stopped at this point, the person may wind up in the psychiatric ward driven out of their mind by imaginary parasites.

Long-term users of crystal meth experience withdrawal when they stop the drug. Withdrawal symptoms include fatigue, depressed mood, loss of pleasurable feelings and suicidal thoughts. Sadly, these symptoms may never go away, even if the person never uses crystal meth again.

Next Jason turned to heroin. Heroin, which is, is also known by the street names of "H", "smack", "skag" and "junk" among other names based upon the geographical area where the drug is used The first step in treating heroin addiction is again, detoxification. It is important to rid the body of the drug to lessen cravings and withdrawal symptoms. It is also important to have medical care to monitor heart rate and blood pressure. With heroin a tolerance is built up requiring the user to use more and more of the drug. If the heroin dose is reduced or use of the drug is stopped, withdrawal symptoms will occur. Regular users may experience initial symptoms of withdrawal within only a few hours after ingesting the last dose. Symptoms of heroin use are: Dry mouth, lethargy, constipation, pupil dilation, and respiratory depression with shallow breathing. Symptoms of heroin withdrawal are: nausea, vomiting, irritability, loss of appetite, runny nose, insomnia, shakiness, muscle cramps, goose bumps, extreme sweating or chills, watery eyes, stomach cramps, and yawning. There is a new treatment now called Meditox. It is a medication and out patient clinic that helps with withdrawal symptoms and allows people to get through the process while maintaining their work or school schedules. Heroin is increasing in purity and decreasing in price making it more attractive to young people. Heroin can be injected, smoked, or sniffed. The injections can be IV or intramuscular. Heroin withdrawal is rarely fatal. Symptoms peak 48 to 72 hours after the last dose and disappear within 7 to 10 days, to be followed by a longer term abstinence syndrome of general malaise and opioid craving.

One reason that I did not believe Jason when he told me he was a heroin addict was that I believed at the time, erroneously, that a heroin addict would always have needle tracks and Jason did not. Only IV users would have needle tracks and the addict might be very cleaver in choosing his injection sites. Also, I thought he was manipulating me to get me to send him another ticket to get back to Seattle. He could always get out of Seattle but could never seem to get back to Seattle.

Currently Jason is committed to staying clean. I asked him if he ever thought about heroin and his response was, "every day of my life". I said, "you don't think you will ever start using again, do you?" He said, "no, no way, I've learned my lesson." Then he went on to tell me about having his impacted wisdom teeth removed. He was in a great deal of pain and very swollen but he would not take the pain medication he was given. "I might like it too much." He said.

8

Overdose Emergency

Eventually Jason was released from the treatment center and returned home. I believe that a treatment center is only as good as their patient's intentions. I don't believe a patient can be helped unless he truly wants to be helped. Jason did not want help. After a couple of months, I came home from work one day and found both Jason missing and money missing from our bedroom. He had left with, his friend; Ryan for a few minutes Phil had discovered the money missing and was hot on his trail. Phil witnessed a probable drug buy when he spotted Jason and Ryan talking to an older man in a beat up truck. He told Jason to get home immediately. He did, and went immediately to his room.

I was angry about the money and I yelled for him to come out into the kitchen, I wanted to talk to him. Neither I nor my husband has ever stolen *any-thing* in our entire lives. Our children were taught that if a dollar was sitting on the counter and it was not yours—leave it alone. I was able to leave money laying around like this all their lives. Now, our own flesh and blood was stealing from us and from his sister. A few minutes later Jason staggered to the kitchen, his eyes glassy, his skin a sickly green. I wondered where he got the grease paint. Scrubbing at his face with a paper towel I realized that it was his skin color. It did not come off. He had actually turned green! About that time, his knees buckled and he collapsed on the floor. He vomited; at that point, I knew it was not alcohol. I called 911. The paramedics arrived in minutes. They called for a special drug unit out of a neighboring town. They started an IV right there on the kitchen floor.

The fire department called ahead to the hospital and transported him all the way to the hospital in their aide car, sirens blaring. He made it but I don't think he appreciated how closely he flirted with death. Nothing but marijuana was found in his blood but I do think it was laced with something that was not tested for. Until then, I believed that you could not overdose on marijuana and I felt that marijuana was actually preferable to alcohol. The flaw in that reasoning is "there is no such thing as an honest drug dealer and you don't know what you are getting besides marijuana." Of course, chronic use makes you lazy and lethargic, saps your ambition and really hampers you in career and/or school. Alcohol is not so great when overused either.

Esperanza family portrait

Jason, home from school in Utah, with Santa, Brandi and a cousin

Jason and our toy poodle

Jason and his mother, Lucinda

Jason in his "Don Johnson" phase

9

High School and Alternative High School

Phil was a key member of the Teamsters Union and was good friends with the current Teamster leader. They went to college together and remained friends all these years. He often did work for the Teamsters and had aspirations of becoming a business agent. After many years of work Phil was offered the position he had sought. However, it occurred in a real time of turmoil in our household. Phil felt that he was just under too much stress to add these new stresses and long hours to his schedule. He was needed at home. Sadly, he turned it down. Had he accepted it, we would be in a far better position in our retirement today.

My blood pressure was high during this period. It magically went down to normal when Jason turned 18. Now he was legally beyond my control and responsibility. I relaxed a bit but I still had a heart attack at age 55. I think that long term stress contributed to this. Phil also went through a period of high blood pressure. We are both healthy now but I am sure we lost a few years of life due to the stress we had been under for such a long time. I no longer cringe when the phone rings and we are no longer waiting for 'the other shoe to drop.'

When Jason was in 10th grade, he was sent to an alternative school. His grades were very poor in regular high school. Carry broke up with him. Jason was devastated but he recovered rather quickly. I soon realized that sending Jason to an alternative school was not in his best interest. I didn't think I had a choice. Now days, parents *do* have a choice and if I had it to do over, I would object. I think that the school district wanted to weed out the low scorers to make their overall test scores seem better. They had given up on him and they wanted to get him out him out of their 'pool' of students. The alternative school did not seem to teach him anything except how to use a condom. Their main curriculum was centered on 'safe sex'. I think it is fine to introduce such subjects but let's not forget the 3 R's. He had a very homely teacher that took a 'way too special' interest in him. This made me very uncomfortable. She wanted to take him in over the Holidays and I was feeling that I was totally loosing control. I couldn't even put my fears of her into words; it was just too horrible and too bizarre. Since that time there have been several teacher/student sex scandals but at the time it was unheard of for a female and I was embarrassed to bring it up to our counselor. Jason had no idea that she had any designs on him and would have been horrified had he known. This was just one reason I felt that Jason needed to be removed from his current environment. His new friend, Ryan, was a terrible influence and came from a terrible home. Ryan's mother lied and covered up for him. I suspected that both of Ryan's parents were alcoholics and Ryan physically abused his parents. The new girl friends he was going to Punk concerts with were obviously into drugs and worse, they had cars. I don't even know where he found these girls-they were of questionable repute. I was frightened for his safety. I felt that I needed to get him away from Ryan and drugs, the sleazy new girl friends, and the strange new teacher right away! I really felt our family was unsafe with Jason in our home as well. My parents agreed with my urgency and we started looking for a program. In the past they had attended town meetings with me, sponsored by our local "Tough Love" group. Our speakers were juvenile judges and lawyers who were also frustrated with Washington's Juvenile Code. The subject of our meetings centered round how to live with our current laws and how to, use them or get around them, until we could get them changed. There were questions from the audience from parents that had sent their children to several other states outside of Washington. Therefore, I had an idea that that was going to be my only alternative too.

10

Hired Kidnapping to Utah

At first I considered Military school and made several phone calls but Military schools want high academic performers. I noticed a few ads in the back of a magazine that my parents received. In fact, my parents pointed it out to me. The school was a long term treatment program. I knew that we were way beyond a quick fix and long term treatment would be necessary. The school empathized education. It was non-denominational but encouraged the kids to attend the church of their choice or of their parent's choice. It was in Utah. By now I didn't care if he became a Mormon. Our church looks upon the Mormon faith as a cult but I have always found their members to be good people. That was not an issue at this point. I called the contact number, thinking that I would shop around a little. I had a very encouraging conversation with the lady who answered the phone and soon I found myself making arrangements. She answered all my concerns. I really did not want to tie him up and transport him in the trunk of my car all the way to Utah. I knew that restraining him would be necessary and that it would be very dangerous to try to restrain him any other way. In spite of all we had been through, we still loved this boy and we did not want to do anything that might hurt him or even *seem* abusive to him. She offered a pick-up service for $5,000. She did say that usually the insurance companies do not pay for the pick-up service. The price sounded fine to me. It solved a lot of problems especially since I was not sure that I could depend on my husband to help me with this or to complete the mission if things got ugly. Phil still was in deep denial and really just wanted to pull the covers up over his head and go into fetal position for the next 10 years or so. He was dead set against sending Jason away. Surprisingly, the insurance company reimbursed me in full for the pick-up fee as well. At one point, Phil said "I get the feeling that I have nothing to say about this." I said, "You know Phil, they didn't even ask for your signature nor did they ask how you felt about it." I know Jason will never forgive me and you probably won't either but I have to do this. I am his mother and I need to save his life." I had the determination of a mother bear fighting for her cub and nothing was going to stop me. It was a decision that did not come easy, though. It was, without a doubt, the hardest and the scariest decision I ever made. I had always been very protective of my children and I had always told them that, "if anybody ever did anything that made them feel uncomfortable then that person would probably also tell them not to tell me. If that ever happens tell me immediately! I will believe you and I will protect you." Now I was turning over custody of one of my children to strangers knowing full well that I was going to ignore any sordid tales that Jason reported to me. I wasn't really sure I could do that. I imagined a child pornography ring being ran out of this school. If Jason only knew of my fears I know he would have used them against me, and I also know I would have been on the next plane to Utah. I don't think, in reality, I could have ignored him. Fortunately, he did not know of my weakness. The plan was for me to get a notarized letter, turning custody over to the school and to secure a hotel room for the two Brigham Young University football players who were coming the night before the pickup. I was scheduled to meet with them and show them where to pick Jason up. These 2 guys were really sweet, soft spoken, gentle giants that immediately put me at ease. I could tell by their questions and their gentle attitude that they were concerned about doing this as easily and as un-traumatic as possible. I told them that Jason had no weapons to my knowledge but that he would fight like he was fighting for his life when they tried to take him. I had taught my children never to allow them selves to be taken to another location. They said they preferred waking him up from a sound sleep to picking him up off the street or at school. Usually a teacher or an observer would call the police if they didn't get to him before he was out of the house. If that should happen, the police will only delay them. It is not against the law to run away in Washington State, and a parent is responsible for their child whether or not they live at home, however, the parent may provide an alternative home for the child of their own choosing. That is what I was doing in providing the letter. The complication to our plan was that Jason was out on run away status at the time. This would be a slight deviation from the plan. I knew where he was, as I usually did. He was living in a boat covered with a canopy in someone's back yard. For food he was going up to the local pizza parlor and snatching pizza off of people's plates and running out. He had been living this way for several days with a friend, Park. Park was from a lovely family and his parents were good friends of ours. Park's parents, our daughter, and my parents were the only people that knew about Jason's scheduled pick-up. Our friends were Mormons in fact, and we were encouraging them to do the same with Park but Park was not self-destructing at the same rate.

As luck would have it, the two boys were discovered in the boat while I was meeting with the Brigham Young University football players. They were evicted by the owners' of the boat. The boys went to Park's house. Park's parents fed the boys a big meal; they took showers and fell sound asleep. As soon as possible his parents called to tell us they had the boys. I still was not home yet from my meeting with the pick-up people. Park's father offered to have the pick-up done at his house. Gratefully, Phil accepted his offer. We were concerned about what kind of uproar that it would cause for the small children of the family to observe, but as it happened it was a quiet and gentle pick-up. At four o'clock in the morning the pick-up people came to the door and introduced themselves, they were shown to the boy's room. "Jason, wake up and put on your boots, you are coming with us," they said. Jason was dazed and confused but he did as he was told. He was walked out to the car and he asked if he was being arrested. "No," they said, "we are going to Utah and it is your choice how we go, we can drive for hours and hours like this or we can fly and be there in a couple of hours. If you choose to fly but you make a scene in the airport, then we get in the car and drive." "I'll fly," he said. After he got in the car he asked if his parents knew they were taking him. He was told that we *hired* them to take him. He asked a few questions on the way but he was mostly in shock. When he got there my contact called me and said, "He's here and what a little dear!" I said, "Bring that kid back immediately; you must have the wrong kid". The next day she called me back to say, "Oh, we got the right kid!" Jason was assigned an around the clock group of counselors who were called "buddies". They stayed with him constantly and when he wore them down the next shift came on duty. As usual Jason could be most charming and polite when it served him best. Kids like this take advantage of their parents and caretakers by wearing them down. Kids typically have more stamina and energy than their parents after a full day of responsibility and it is easy for them to wear their parents down. When that happens at the school they just change shifts. Everybody has survival needs. Parents need to sleep just like anyone else. It is not possible to watch a child 24 hours a day. There will be a time that the child can sneak out of the house and do whatever he wants. Child Protective Service will not allow you to chain your child to the bed at night, not that you would want to. Therefore, it does not make sense to make the already harassed parent responsible for curfew laws, or school truancy. A kid like this would love seeing their parent go to jail for something *they* did. By the same token, a physically abused child tries to hide it from teachers, doctors and authority figures. They don't belligerently march in and announce it to their principal. That kind of behavior has "lie" written all over it. Child Protective Service needs to get some child behavior and psychology training. I was so upset by the way our son's case was handled and at the same time, sickened by newspaper accounts of the dozens of helpless children who were being tortured to death at the hands of their care takers, that I became a CASA volunteer (Court Appointed Special Advocate). They are so overloaded with cases. I have a new appreciation for the caseworkers, CASAs, lawyers, and judges. They are really good people doing a really thankless job with not enough time, not enough money, not enough resources. They are doing a huge service for a huge number of people within the constraints of a less than perfect legal system. They are also bound by that legal system. Even one child failing to be protected is too many. It is horrible but it happens.

While away at school in Utah Jason did well in school. They immediately cut his Mohawk into a still strange looking haircut and enforced a strict dress code. Not more than one black item of clothing, no jewelry for boys, no offensive T-shirts, and so on. He learned to earn privileges with good behavior but only long enough to allow him an opportunity to run away. It was different when he ran away in Utah. We did not have the same fears of our insurance dropping us for unauthorized leave. The whole town turned out for the search party, he would only be gone for a matter of hours. He was easy to spot due to his haircut and dress. The townspeople were familiar with the "look" and he was immediately caught. Only once did he make it to another town and was picked up at a bus station. The Brigham Young University football players just walked up to him, said his name, Jason stood up and put his hands behind his back to await the handcuffs.

During this time our family went on a family reunion cruise that Jason had to earn the privilege to go on. He was doing really well up until he decided to leave his classroom to go to the restroom. He met a girl in the boy's restroom and they were caught having sex in the boy's restroom. About that time, one of his drug using girlfriends from Washington wrote to him that she was pregnant and he totally fell apart. Surprisingly, he was concerned about her drug use and what that might do to an innocent life. As it turned out, the pregnancy was a lie and it only served to upset him and other girls that he was involved with. I will have to say that Jason, although extremely sexually active, must be extremely responsible about his reproductive life. To my knowledge he has never gotten anyone pregnant. His behavior took a turn for the worse, at this point, and he was not allowed to go with us on the cruise. He was there for over two years and he managed to run away maybe four times but never overnight. He got a job while he was there. He moved off campus and into a house with a group of counselors and kids. They learned to operate a household, on a budget. They planned menus, shopped for groceries, cooked for the group, maintained the house, and also bred and raised rabbits. Jason really got a lot from this experience. It did not entirely make up for those years that a teenager is prepared for life on their own by their parents but it really helped. Jason took drivers training while he was there twice and failed both times. He also took it once in a Washington high school and failed and once in Job Corp and failed. He really had no interest in driving. I felt that this was a necessary step in becoming independent so I was willing to pay for it however many times it took. He never successfully passed a drivers training class until he was in his mid-20s. I think that was because *I* wanted him to drive, not him. He won't admit it, and the evidence was not immediate, but I think he learned some skills that he later used to get back on the right track.

11

Coming Home and Into Job Corp

Jason was now getting close to 18. At age 18 the school in Utah had to release him. He still hadn't graduated and I was still desperate to get him educated, at least through high school and with a vocation so he would be able to support himself. There was no way that he had time to earn his diploma at this point. We certainly do not meet the low income requirement making him eligible for Job Corp, but it was looking like a really good vocational program to me and they also earn their GED. I wrote to two of my congressmen and explained my situation. I explained that I realized that I did not meet the low income requirement but pleaded for special consideration. One never responded at all and the other not only responded but assigned an aide, to see that I had everything I needed. He had the head of Job Corp near us call me and make arrangements. I offered Jason an early out of Utah (three months) if he would go right into Job Corp. He agreed. He chose food service. That did not work out. He had become incredibly even more sloppy and unsanitary from his intermittent life on the street. Next he chose carpentry. His instructor called me and said he was really too disorganized for carpentry and his math skills were to poor. I thought that the deck hand program might work for him. He was always talking about going commercial fishing in Alaska. He was now not interested in that. He stayed for a few weeks. Complained that he didn't like the music they played, really crucial things like that, and he left. He came home and was told that he would have to get a job immediately. He was not allowed to lie around the house while everybody else worked or went to school. He got up one morning and took the bus into Seattle. He came home saying he had a job at a pizza store. The next day he took the bus again on the pretense of going to work and we didn't see or hear from him for two years. I have often wondered why he would choose this inconsiderate manner in which to disappear. We would not have tried to prevent him from leaving at this point. Our daughter remembers how relieved she felt when he didn't come home and remembers how shocked her friends and neighbors were that she wasn't worried. We had become accustomed to living our lives without concern on some level.

12

Beginning of Full Time Street Life

I know that I had actually resolved myself to our son dying very young. I still cared very much but it was really out of my hands at this point. I had spent a good number of years fighting desperately to save him, and now he was 18 and it was truly out of my hands. There came a peace that I had not felt in years, when he turned 18. I had played the dreaded event over and over in my mind and actually resolved myself to it. Jason lived mainly in the university district for the next 4 years, raising hell, inciting riots and using drugs and alcohol, leading or participating in every demonstration or protest available. My greatest fear was that he would fall into prostitution. He was little, baby faced and cute, a perfect target. My counselor relieved some of my fears by pointing out that he was not that type of kid and that he stayed dirty and smelly to keep the pedophiles away. Looking back, I don't think Jason or any of his long term girl friends ever got into prostitution. Another big fear was what would happen to him in jail. However, he spent time in jail, never doing hard time in prison. These are two very different places. Jail soon became a welcome event for me. At least I knew where he was and that he was warm and well fed and probably safer than homeless on the street. I told him that I would never visit him in jail or in prison. I told him that, "You have the right to self destruct but I have the right not to watch." I held to that promise. Of course my worse fear was a drug overdose, disease, or violence on the street. Still, when it was rainy and cold, I couldn't help wondering where he was and if he was warm and dry.

He got beat up in New York on his 21st birthday and got his nose broken. It was a racist skin head that attacked him. He recognized Jason from a civil rights demonstration. Surprisingly, the emergency room doctors fixed his nose up really well. Jason is not nearly as attractive as he used to be and he has aged at a far faster rate but his nose looks good. His teeth were really beautiful. He went for years not brushing and not having regular dental care. Also the use of amphetamines is really detrimental to your oral health. I thought he would be toothless by now. Fortunately, he had really good teeth and they withstood life on the streets and drug abuse. He now takes really good care of his teeth and they are in great shape, with the exception of the problem he has with his two lower front teeth. He has lost an extreme amount of bone support in that area and is about to loose two teeth. His dentist claims to never have seen such a case (he does not know about Jason's past life on the street or his past drug use). Jason is trying really hard to save them.

Actually, he managed to get good medical care while homeless. One day, long after he turned 18, I got a call from the University of Washington hospital. The lady calling was trying to collect on a hospital emergency room bill. Apparently he had been brought there by an aide car. I asked if it was for a drug overdose. "Oh I can't tell you what it is for I am bound by privacy laws", she said. "Well then can you tell me what services the charges are for", I asked. "Oh No, I can't tell you that either that would fall under our privacy laws." I see," I said, "so you want me to pay for something that I had no idea I had bought, and you won't tell me what it is for … Humm, I don't think I want to pay for that!" "Don't you want to protect your son's credit!" she exclaimed. I replied "He is a drug addict, Lady; his credit score is way down on my list of priorities for him!!" I never heard from that hospital again.

We tried to stay in contact with him by networking the street kids when we needed to get a message to him. Phil could usually find him. He would often encounter a street kid and ask him if he wanted to go get a pizza. He would tell the street kid that he understood that it was against their code of ethics to inform on another kid's whereabouts, but could he get a message to Jason to call home. A few days later Jason would call. Seattle is a very homeless friendly sort of place. The weather is mild and the restaurants feed them, they have places to do your laundry, get free medical attention get new clothes, and to pick up bags of groceries. You can ride the downtown buses all day for free and there are twice the services for teenagers. Seattle is a very liberal city. A group of churches in the university district operate "Teen Feed" in a church basement. A good meal is provided 2 or 3 times a week and there are Christian counselors at each table to talk to the kids. The kids really like it and it has become a meeting place for the kids. The kids show their appreciation by complaining that they don't provide vegetarian dishes. I always felt that these organizations were just enabling these kids to be out there and felt that if the feeding stations did not exist the kids would get hungry and go home. I used to call the minister that ran this operation and complain about that. He was very nice and talked to me at length. He understood my point of view but said there were some out there that were there due to abuse. He agreed that they were in the minority but those are the kids that they were trying to help. He had to accept all the kids that showed up for "teen feed". Jason was a guest on a radio talk show once discussing the homeless problem. The minister and I were guests on the same show the next week discussing an opposing view.

During this time Jason was in and out of jail mostly for being drunk in public, unlawful demonstrations, vagrancy, criminal trespass (sleeping in an abandoned building), and loitering. The business owners did not like the homeless kids hanging out in front of their businesses so they pressured the police, who in turn hasseled the kids. Often he would be asked for ID. His ID would not be returned to him. The next day he would be arrested for not having any ID on him. One day he was drunk on the street when he saw a police officer on the other side of the street who had taken his ID the day before. He started yelling at the police officer to give him back his ID. Suddenly an arm came out of the door he was standing in front of and pulled him inside. It was a University student who was 'rescuing' him from a "drunk in public" arrest. He had never seen this person before but she apparently liked him and kept him a few days. She soon became his worse nightmare and his stalker.

This girl's parents must have had money because she was a university of Washington student who lived off campus in her own apartment and seemed to be able to fly all over the country looking for Jason. She was definitely not a street kid but perhaps a wannabe and was able to network them and find out Jason's whereabouts. His friends soon learned that she was an unwelcome stalker and refused to tell her where he was. Her next tactic was to call his family on the pretense of having *information*. Once she had us on the phone, she would try to draw out any knowledge that we had and then put the pieces together. Jason rode the rails from Seattle to New York to get away from her. She actually found him in New York! We really knew her game by now and became skillful in not falling into her trap. This went on for months and finally she called and got Brandi on the phone. "Did you hear? She asked, excitedly, "Jason overdosed and he is in the hospital." This was not true. Brandi's quick response was, "Yes, isn't it sad … He died." We never heard from her again and it's my guess, neither did Jason.

Jason was now over 21 and professing to be getting weary of the street life. Actually the services available to him at this age are fewer and fewer. He did not want to go to homeless shelters because he was intimidated by the "bums." I wondered what he thought the next step for a street kid was if it was not to be a "bum". He started talking about getting a construction job but it was really hard for him because he did not have transportation nor did he have a driver's license, an address or a phone number. We thought we would try again. We set him up at the YMCA in down town Seattle and paid his rent for 2 months. Bought him clothes, food and set up appointments with prospective employers. Phil hooked him up with our Teamster contacts and instructed him to have a job before we return from vacation. We left for 6 weeks in Mexico. When we returned, Phil went to the YMCA to check on him. He was still sleeping and hung over at 11 AM. He had not done a single interview. His rent was due and Phil refused to pay it. I am so proud of Phil for being so strong. It really is out of character for Phil to be so strong where Jason is concerned. Sadly, Jason did not make any effort to complete his end of the bargain. Phil helped him put his belongings into a garbage bag and dropped him off in a park. It was a heartbreaking day and Phil still gets tears in his eyes when he talks about it.

During the course of his homeless life he sold everything he had, probably for pennies on the dollar. First his coveted leather jacket went, then his guitar, then his stereo and his collection of records and CDs. I bought him several pairs of Doc Marten high top boots that were very expensive and warm jackets. The next time I would see him he would be wearing $5 slip on vans and a hooded sweat-shirt. At one point, while I was attempting another rescue and paying his rent, I bought him a computer so he could work on his GED. I don't know what happened to that. He no longer has it. Surprisingly, and contrary to many educators' opinions, he was able to get his GED and he did it rather easily and quickly once he put his mind to it.

I think silliest thing that concerned me while he was on the street, was the damage that must be happening to his self esteem. Knowing how citizens, shop owners and the police treated him like garbage broke my heart. I had always guarded his self esteem with vigilance and now he was putting himself in the position to be verbally and sometimes physically abused on a daily basis. I told myself that it was his choice and that it was a logical consequence to his own behavior, but I still worried that it would cause permanent damage. Surprisingly, it did not seem to.

13

Tragedies and Rescues

There existed, what the kids called, "The Big Green Machine". It was a bus that apparently ran up and down the west coast. It was run by what they called a "bunch of really cool hippies". It was a cheap way to travel. As a result, large groups of university district homeless street kids often went to Los Angeles or San Francisco for several months at a time. It was on one of these trips to Los Angeles that Jason made an urgent phone call home. He told his sister that someone was trying to kill him and he had to get out of LA fast! Apparently he was hanging out around Grauman's Chinese Theater, posing for pictures for $5 each. The tourists were happy to get a picture of this odd boy with a multi colored super spiked up Mohawk and spikes all over his clothes. He looked very strange and scary but was surprisingly friendly and accommodating. Coincidentally, we were visiting Phil's sister in Los Angeles and had just spent the day in that very area. In fact, we were in that area when he called. We waited for him to call back. He told us that he was living in a house (I suspect it was a meth lab) with some prostitutes and drug dealers and he had come up short. Apparently he was selling for them and something happened to the money he was suppose to come back with. According to him, he was already in bad favor with his housemates for jumping in to protect a prostitute who was being beaten up by her pimp. He said he was sure they were going to kill him. It was probably a manipulative lie but we could not chance it. He put on a great act if it was a lie but he was always a very talented actor. It was getting dark now and it was a long drive back to the Sunset Strip area from Huntington Beach. He told us where to meet him and we stopped to ask directions from another older street person. He gave us directions and then said, "but buddy, I wouldn't even go in there" It was definitely a really seedy area. Street people were lying on every bench. Drunks were staggering down the street everywhere you looked. I got out and started peeking under all the newspapers covering the faces of the sleeping street people and looking down allies while Phil drove really slowly down the street. I called out Jason's name. There was not a policeman in sight. Suddenly, Jason appeared out of the shadows and jumped into the back seat. He ducked down and Phil sped out of the area. It was not until we got to the freeway that Jason sat up. He had a very strange and noxious odor about him, an odor I had never smelled before. It was so offensive that I fed him and allowed him to shower at his Aunt and Uncle's house but then made him sleep in the car. The next morning I took him to a bus station and bought him a ticket to Seattle. I don't believe he ever went back to Los Angeles. I don't know to this day the real or complete story on that incident.

While he was on yet another trip to San Francisco I got a 2 AM phone call, collect. I usually don't answer late night phone calls—it is usually a wrong number—but something just told me to answer. This is a sense I have had before and because of it I have never failed to answer an emergency phone call. It was Jason and he said, "Mom, I just want to tell you good bye and you will probably never hear from me or see me again. I want you to know that all this stuff that I have gotten into was not your fault, it was all me, I did it all to myself. Tell Dad too. I am sorry and I love you both." Well, I am wide awake now, and not knowing if I am dealing with a suicide threat or what. He sounded clear headed and not on drugs and I kept trying to find out where he was and what was going on. He was very vague but he said he had done someone wrong and some mutual friends tricked him into coming over to their apartment and he was being held there until the party he offended came over. They were probably going to kill him and he deserved it. They allowed him to use the phone for just a minute to say good-bye to his parents. I could hear people in the background yelling for him to get off the phone and finally he hung up. I immediately called the operator and asked for the phone number and address of the collect call that I had just received. She told me that she did not have access to that information and that I would have to wait for my next bill. I told her the whole drawn out sob story. She apologized but still she claimed not the have that information. I was ready to hop a plane to San Francisco and hurt someone. Now I would have to wait 3 weeks to get my bill. For one week I repeatedly called all the hospitals, the morgues and police stations in the greater San Francisco area and there was no John Doe that met his description. I left his description and my name and number. The Police officers all told me that it was probably just a paranoid episode caused by coming down from drugs and that everything was probably fine. They see this all the time. They too, took his description down and my phone number. I worried for 3 weeks and then got my phone bill. I called the San Francisco number. It turned out to be a drop in station for homeless people to shower and get cleaned up. I didn't hear from him again for year or so. The next time I talked to him, I asked him why he did that to me. At first he acted like he didn't remember doing that, then he brushed it off and said, "they just roughed him up a little."

It was not uncommon to get calls from him saying that he woke up with 'gunk' dried all inside his pants, he has blisters all over his genitals and it really hurts to pee. The girl he was seeing left town and didn't tell anybody she was leaving. I told him, "She may not have said goodbye but she gave you multiple gifts before she left. Go to the doctor immediately." Often he would get very sick with respiratory problems out on the street and he would come home to recover. I would tell him that it was not fair for us to be exposed to all these street diseases that he brings home to us. We do not live our lives like that and we should not have to deal with this. However, I would still take him in. How could I not? On one occasion I picked him up right off the street and I took him directly to my doctor. I was so embarrassed but so impressed with how she treated this filthy boy without ever hesitating. She treated him with dignity in spite of it all. She did tell him that if he didn't stop snorting drugs he was going to loose his nose. He had already burned a hole through his septum.

When he was little and he would get sick in the middle of the night, he would run to me. I had a permanent vomit stain on the carpet next to my bed. Even as a small child, our daughter would run to the bathroom and then call me but not Jason, even as a teenager. It was the same with emotional trauma, until very recently, even at 30 years old. I could always expect a call if he was hurting in any way. I believe that his failure to keep in contact now is his way of saying, "I don't need you any more. I have finally grown up."

It was on yet another of these trips to San Francisco that a large group of kids found a "squat". A squat is an abandoned or even condemned building that homeless people move into. They make it appear secured, often by boarding up entrances themselves while leaving a secret place for them selves to enter. Often they re-start the power to the building. That is what they did here. Now they can only use the center core of the building so the lights can't be seen from the street. It takes the power company a while to notice that power is being drawn to this building and even longer to investigate. Jason and his current girl friend lived together on the 9th floor. To get to the 9th floor they had to climb the stairs counting the floors in the dark. On the 9th floor there were boards over the empty elevator shaft that they had to walk across in the dark. One night all the kids had gathered at another location to party. Jason's girl friend was feeling like she had overdone the drugs, alcohol or a combination of the two and decided to return to their squat while she still could. She left alone. A few minutes later, Jason got concerned enough to follow her. He was shocked to find her lying unconscious at the bottom of the elevator shaft. She had miscounted the flights of stairs and stepped into the empty elevator shaft. She fell 9 stories and through the top of the elevator car which was sitting at the bottom of the shaft. Jason got help and showed the aide people how to gain entrance to the squat. She broke many bones and was paralyzed and unconscious. After months in the hospital she started rehab. Eventually, she was sent her back to Minneapolis Saint Paul where her parents were. There she continued rehab. When she left San Francisco she was in an automated wheel chair and could operate it when wearing special gloves. Jason stays in touch with her still today, he says she is his best friend and always will be. Today she is a librarian. She is still paralyzed. I believe that she lives independently and supports herself. I believe she encourages Jason to make something of his life. I talked to her at least once on the phone. She seems to be a really sweet girl. It is no wonder that Jason cares so much about her. Jason stayed by her side at the hospital while she fought for life. At first the hospital personnel did not approve of this dirty smelly person hanging around the hospital. She would call out for him in her delirium. It was such a fight for her to live that the medical people changed their attitude towards Jason and actually encouraged him to stay. The night that the accident occurred, we received a hysterical sobbing phone call from Jason. I had never heard him so distraught. My heart bled for him and for her. I received almost daily calls from him. He only got a little less sad. He reported that all the other kids went back to Seattle, their squat now compromised and therefore, useless. He seemed to feel so alone and so sad.

Because of the extreme trauma that he experienced and the frequent phone calls, I felt that this was his "rock bottom," the life changing event that might turn him around. He always seemed to be able to travel all over the country but he was rarely able to get back home. I had frequently pointed this out to him and reminded him that "I no longer did rescues or return trips". In actuality, I did often pay for return trips but each time made him wait and suffer a little longer. I waited and watched as he tried to get back to Seattle. I now felt certain that this event was going to be his "life altering event". Phil set up some interview appointments for him. We found an apartment on the bus line for him. I got the bus schedule on-line and kept it handy. One evening when he called me I told him about the apartment and about the interviews and asked him if he was willing to change his life. He assured me that he was willing.

It probably seems that I gave a lot of "no-more" warnings and performed a lot of repeated failed rescues. Then I went right back and tried it again. It is very difficult to know where to draw the line between empowering and enabling. I don't profess to be an expert on which is which. I do know I have made a lot of mistakes. The fear that your child is going to get trapped in the backwaters and never escape is so great. The danger is so real. When he was trying to induce me to pay for a ticket back to Seattle, he told me that, "San Francisco was bringing him down" that he was using heroin, he was in a really bad environment and that he needed to get out of there. I didn't believe that he ever used heroin. I recognized that as a manipulative ploy from the beginning. That was proven to me when he spent some time in jail and he never went through withdrawal. Still, it was at this point that I told him to walk to the bus depot, tell the man behind the counter your name, and there will be a ticket waiting for you. I then immediately called the bus depot and purchased a ticket with my charge card. It was late and the man that answered the phone was just closing up after finishing the ticket sales for that day. He was kind enough to re-open to sell me the ticket and then to wait for Jason to arrive. Jason went straight to the bus depot, leaving all his belongings behind. There was a bad snow storm in the Sisques and the bus was delayed several hours in the mountains of Oregon. Jason was without food, money or a coat on this trip. When I picked him up we went straight to Denny's. I really did not know how to feed him. I knew that he had found it necessary to further complicate his homeless lifestyle by becoming vegetarian. This makes jail very difficult also. Jail kitchens do not cater to alternative diets. It is a mystery to me that so many street kids adopt this life style. It makes it really difficult for the social service people who are trying to feed them. Jason was famished and shivering from the cold damp weather. He was actually pleasant to be with and seemed grateful to be home.

The next day we took him to show him the apartment that we arranged for him to move into. The owners of the apartment took one look at him and backed out of the agreement. For years he was unable to see how the way he looked made a statement to people. Yes, it was his right to dress and wear his hair however he wanted but other people had a right to withdraw from you and judge you in response. Whether or not it is fair or not is really not the issue. It was very difficult for him to get a place to live for many years. It took us, taking him around to look at apartments to kind of balance the way he looked. Occasionally, we would find an apartment that looked as bad and he did and it would be a match. For all the hard work in finding a place, you would think he would value that, but it wasn't long before he was evicted and we would start the whole process over. Searching for an apartment without a good track record or a job only further complicates and shrinks the pool of prospective dwellings. Also, needing the rent to be next to nothing and on the bus line further complicates it. Getting a job without an address or a phone number and without a place to clean up is next to impossible. He now had green dread locks which he refused to cut off. He wore a studded collar and wrist cuffs and chains hanging from his belt. None of this makes you model tenant *or* employee material. I did not even realize that some of the type of apartments that he got even existed. They can be horrible but they are inner city and still far from cheap.

I don't remember what he went to jail for. Phil thinks it was for being a passenger in a car and not wearing a seat belt then not paying the fine. I think it was for loitering in the University District and not paying the fine. I do recall that it was a harassment issue on the part of the arresting officer, and that it was a "trumped-up" charge. I went to court and sat quietly watching. Afterwards his attorney was surprised to discover that I was even there. He said that Jason could avoid the jail time if I would only pay the $15 fine. I refused and the attorney was dumbfounded. He made some sort of statement about my ability to afford it. I pointed out that that was certainly not the issue and that I had paid more than that to park my car that day. What I wanted Jason to realize is that if you present yourself as he does and you hang out in front of businesses, those businesses may be affected. The business owners are then going to put pressure on the police and they are going to put pressure on the kids. Yes, they have a right. No, it is not fair, but that is the way it is. By choosing their lifestyle they choose the way they are treated. I did not choose that lifestyle so I should not suffer for their choice. Evidently, they must experience being unfairly imprisoned as well. They must not be tired enough of it to decide to change their life style. It is the same old thing I have been trying to teach him from day one. "You choose the behavior you choose the consequence." I have been religious about following through on that. He was to into drugs and alcohol to make logical decisions.

After hanging out on the streets of Seattle for a while he met another street kid, a girl named Jenny. They decided to relocate to Portland Oregon. Perhaps the police were becoming too much of a problem for them. On the day he was supposed to leave with Jenny, he was arrested again. I got an urgent collect call from Jason in jail. Even local calls from jail are always collect. He requested that I call a drop-in center and have someone put a note on the bulletin board for 'Jenny, with the green and purple hair." "Don't leave, I'm in jail. Wait for me. I'll be out in a day or so, Jason". Jenny got the message and she did wait for him. It was the beginning of a very long and seemingly good relationship. It lasted probably about 12 years. Jenny came from a family very much like ours; a two-parent, upper middle class family; she had three sisters, all of whom were achievers. She seemed to have a close relationship with them. One of her sisters studied abroad, and another was a journalist. Jenny was smart and had ambitious dreams but they were just dreams. She never really took the steps necessary to achieve them. She often took college classes but never worked towards anything marketable. She had less ambition than Jason. Jason said Jenny was depressed and therefore on disability. Jason was kind, respectful, and loving towards her. I found her to be a little selfish and less thoughtful towards him but that's a Mother's point of view. She was very sweet and likeable. They went to Portland for several months and found it more difficult to be a street person there. You have to have a utility receipt to buy beer or alcohol in Portland. The police are on horseback in Portland. Jason has always been intimidated by large animals. Eventually, they returned to Seattle. Jason became active in a campaign to house the homeless.

I was surprised to see his picture and the text of a speech he gave to a committee studying this issue in the Seattle Times. I was also surprised that he used an alias. He had become increasingly paranoid about privacy issues. He does not want anyone to know his address, phone number or even his real name. He gives out our address and phone number instead of his own still today. He never leaves a forwarding address when he changes residences. I do not know how to reach him today. Eventually Jason and Jenny each got a room in a low cost housing project near the Grey line bus depot in Seattle. I think that Jason got this because he was active in getting the city to fund it. It had strict rules regarding the requirement of holding or searching for a job and the shared maintenance of the building. It had a big common kitchen and common bathrooms.

It was while Jason and Jenny lived here that Brandi got married. Brandi married a Marine and had a big beautiful military wedding. We had planned this wedding for 2 years and every detail was top notch. She had never given us any trouble and endured plenty of hardships due to our preoccupation with Jason. She was our only daughter. We felt she deserved the nicest of weddings. There was no way that I was going to allow Jason to ruin this happy day for her. He kept asking when it was going to be and I kept lying. I told him it was going to be on a military base and I didn't know yet. I thought that his distaste for the military would discourage him. I told him that we had to wait for the chaplain's schedule. Jason proclaimed to be an atheist so a religious service might discourage him. Finally, he said in frustration, "Mom, I *have* to go to my sister's wedding! If I don't I can never go back and do it again!" I said, "Alright but I will not allow you to ruin this for her. There will be no anti-military or anti-religious demonstrations or even so much as eye rolling, you will wear a tux and have your hair cut to my specifications. This is absolutely non negotiable. If there is any disturbance of any kind the police will be called and you will be removed." He said, "Mom, I can't believe that you think I would ruin my sister's wedding! Can

Jenny come too?" I said "yes but the same rules go for her. I will buy her an appropriate dress." I got perfect cooperation from them both. Brandi and I picked them up and took them to the tux shop. We walked in and I told the young clerk that I needed to add one more to the tux list for our wedding. The young man just stood there staring at Jason in his punked out attire. "My brother needs to be fitted for a tux," Brandi repeated firmly. "Don't you need to write that down and take some measurements," I asked. "Oh, yes," he responded but he couldn't seem to function in the presence of Jason. An older man came to the rescue and he was not at all affected by Jason's bizarre appearance. He began taking measurements and calling them out to the young man who was still standing there with his mouth open in shocked disbelief. "Shouldn't you write this down?" I asked. We also fitted him with shoes. His Dock Martin-to the knee boots-just wouldn't work. Next we took Jenny shopping. We found a beautiful pink dress that fit her perfectly. She looked lovely in it. I didn't ask her if she liked it, I knew she would only wear it once. I was surprised to see that Jenny had a great figure that she kept hidden under big sloppy clothes. She also needed a new bra. She only had a black one which would not work under her pink dress. She was a tiny slim girl but with big enough breasts that she needed an under wire bra. We got dyed to match shoes for her and we were all set. We had lunch and I took them home. On the day of the wedding, Phil picked up Jason and Jenny a few hours before the wedding because we had to have pictures taken. They came in their street clothes and I brought all their wedding clothes with me. Jason walked into the beautiful facility and was immediately intimidated. I told him and Jenny to go up stairs and change into their wedding clothes and they would feel better. Eventually Jason started to relax. It was difficult to tell with Jenny. No one at the wedding would dare to treat him anyway but welcoming and friendly, they were our friends of many years and they had held our hands through many a crisis. Many relatives had not seen him for years and were thrilled to see him again. Jason and Jenny sat right in front and Jason sobbed throughout the entire ceremony. They really seemed to enjoy the whole affair. We had to end the event at 11 PM so at about 10 PM we had them change back into their street clothes and had the stretch limo driver drive them home. They really didn't want to leave then, they were enjoying it so much, but we were to busy to drive them and we were already paying the limo driver so it made perfect sense to do it that way. We got some wonderful pictures which I still treasure. I sent a good picture of Jason and Jenny to her parents. She is such a pretty girl. It is really a shame that she doesn't take more pride in her appearance. We are so glad that we included Jason and Jenny and so is Brandi. Our only regret is that we didn't tell the groom that

Jason would be there. The groom had been deployed for several months and when he left we were all adamant in not allowing Jason to attend. This is the first time the groom had been home in all that time. He wasn't even able to attend the rehearsal so he had to be coached by his attendants occasionally. When we changed our minds, we neglected to tell the groom. When he saw Jason there he immediately got angry. He did not know how this came about and he was really shocked and surprised. It was really wrong for us to change the plan without informing him. It was the only time that the groom had ever seen Jason but he recognized him by his pictures immediately.

Jason is not fond of rules and it wasn't long until he was evicted from his low cost housing arrangement in Seattle. They were able to get a really old and run down apartment in the Central District where they stayed for several months. They both were finally getting tired of living this life style and Jason was looking for a way to make an honest living. Once again Phil called upon his union contacts and found that there were several job possibilities in the South end. Not having transportation or a drivers license was a problem. We took them apartment shopping once again and found a fairly nice apartment near Kent, a southern suburb. Rent was cheaper here and the units much nicer. Phil again lined up some interviews but Jason managed not to land any of them. Our dear friend, the head of the Northwest Teamsters Union, counseled Jason about how to dress and what it takes to land and hold a job. I think that Jason recalled this counseling and, when he was *really* ready, put it into practice. At a later date, I was to be very pleased at the turn-around that Jason was to make in his work ethic. At this time, transportation being the problem that it was, Jason was only able to get little local part-time jobs at restraunts. I made the decision to give him drivers training AGAIN. I hired Sears's driving school. They would go and pick him up at his apartment and do his training in their cars. They were very expensive, especially for adults, but very good. They even did his practice sessions and took him to the department of motor vehicles to get his license. This time he really wanted to get his license and I feel he is a very good driver today. I told him to always maintain his license whether or not he is driving. It was too hard to get it to let it lapse. Jenny was not encouraging. I know she once had a driver's license but something happened and she lost it. She remarked, "You have no idea the grief that a license will bring you!" I felt that it was a crucial part of becoming independent. It was only about a year until Jenny wanted to go back to Portland. Jason said he wanted to go to school in a program that would teach him how to maintain refrigeration and heating plants, it was near Portland. He really had gathered information on this and convinced me that he was serious and that it would be a good thing to get into. I felt that it would be a good thing to have Jason another state away from us. In retrospect, I don't think he had any plans to go to school. I think that Jenny just wanted to move further south. I took Jason and Jenny to Portland to apartment shop.

14

The Move to Portland, Getting a GED and Becoming a Carpenter

We found an apartment in a nice neighborhood that was near down town and was walking distance to everything. The price was right. What we didn't know, was that the managers were brother and sister psychopaths! I am talking serious, institutional type mental illness here. I paid first and last months rent, damage deposit, Jenny and Jason paid what they could and we all went back to Seattle to get ready for the move. We cautioned Jason that he would need to line up friends to help load because we were just too old to do that any more. He assured us that he would. Moving day arrived. We arrived. His friends did NOT arrive. We had no choice but to load up and head for Portland. We got our first taste of the psychopathic rage of "brother manager" shortly after we arrived. The parking lot was about half full and we would be constantly with the van, so we parked it in the closest spot and started unloading. We had just taken our first load up the steps to the second story apartment when this insane old man came running out wildly, waving his arms and yelling something. It was not immediately clear what the emergency was. He was acting like a 2 year old having a tantrum. We stared at him in confusion and disbelief. Apparently, the problem was that we were parked in the wrong spot. When we finally understood that, Phil said, "OK, I'll move it in a minute". Oh no, another explosion. That only enraged him further. I'm afraid I might have laughed. I didn't mean too, it's just that I have never seen someone treat an empty parking space like a dog with a big juicy bone. Perhaps if he had just told us where we COULD park rather than where we could NOT park we could be more accommodating. Little did we know what was in store for us all. Jason and Jenny lived here for a couple of years. They both quit smoking and Jason gave up marijuana too. He wanted very much to hold a job and drug testing discourages that. Jenny continued the marijuana. I did not know until later that Jenny was still using marijuana. Perhaps the manager smelled it at some point. I thought he acted really silly sneaking around the apartment looking through windows at house plants and asking questions about plants that looked nothing like marijuana.

Jason was able to get a job at Saint Vincent De Paul in a manufacturing shop. He learned to use tools and gained some skills there. They hired a small group of handicapped people to do small tasks there also. Jason was so gentle and kind to these people that they put him in charge of helping them learn to adapt their handicap to the use of their tools. He really became attached to these people and wanted to see them included as regular employees. When they had a company picnic he discovered that this group was not invited. This incensed Jason. He wanted to know why. They are part of our staff too, he argued. It is too much trouble, he was told. Who will watch them? I will, he volunteered. One day one of these employees kept taking her shoes off. Jason was told that it was a safety issue and he must make her keep her shoes on. Finally, he asked her why she takes her shoes off. She complained that her shoes hurt her. He looked at her feet and her toenails had grown around and were puncturing her foot. This infuriated Jason. He immediately got on the phone to the "house" where she lived aren't you people supposed to take care of her and make sure that she is healthy and all her needs are met? He asked. They answered in the affirmative. "Then why are her toenails growing into her foot? Don't you notice that she can hardly walk? That is just plain neglect!" he shouted. "I am turning in a report!" Obviously, going through the proper channels never met anything to Jason and he got called on the carpet for these two incidents. His sense of justice has always gotten him into trouble. They probably threatened to fire him but they didn't. He was also trying to organize a labor union there and he certainly was no longer in good favor. They did lay him off at the first opportunity.

He went to night school and got his GED. He signed up with the carpenters union. They put him on the waiting list as an apprentice carpenter. Jenny was pressuring him to have a baby. Jason refused. "I can't even take care of myself," he said. Jenny went to California on the pretense of visiting her parents at Christmas time and returned on New Years Eve. This is something she did every year alone. Jason said she was really affectionate to him upon her return but she awoke him in the middle of the night to say she was leaving the next day. He was devastated. She called her mother and arranged to have some of her stuff shipped to California. Her mother was shocked and surprised too. Actually she did not stay with her parents and I doubt that her mother saw too much of her over Christmas. Jason and Jenny both cried and cried but Jason suspected that she was having a relationship with his so called "best friend". I suspect she was already pregnant. Jenny and Jason's former "friend" now have a toddler together. Jason is still furious at his "friend". I am grateful that Jenny did not try to tell Jason that the baby was his. Jason is really faithful to his girlfriends that he is in a relationship with but if he is not in a relationship it is a sexual free for all. I know that he would leave his current relationship before he would enter into another relationship. His friends' girlfriends are strictly off limits. All of his relationships have ended in tragedy. He now says he will never let another girl live with him. He really does not have time for a girlfriend he works really long hours seven days a week and he is out of town most of the time.

Jason went through a period of self blame and sadness over the loss of Jenny. He called me often and wanted to talk about the "why" of it. He kept asking if I thought he treated her well and asked if I thought he could have done better. I told him he was smart to refuse to have a baby. He could be burdened with child support payments and have a child that was in another state that he doesn't even get to see. She took half of their meager assets and I am sure she did not contribute half to their acquisition. I did not tell him, but I felt he was better off without Jenny, although, I felt his pain deeply.

I realized that not having a car was a real handicap for him. I felt more comfortable getting him one now that Jenny was gone. I did not know about her driving history, but I did know that she did have a history. It worried me. I went to Portland and purchased him a used small car and car insurance for 1 year. I made sure that my name was not tied to that car in any way. I paid cash for the car and stressed that I wanted to purchase the car anonymously. I drove the car to his apartment and parked it right outside Jason's apartment. Being from Washington, I did not know Oregon motor vehicles laws. I noticed that there was no sticker in the back window and I questioned the dealer about the procedure for getting it licensed. I must admit that I was not functioning with a clear mind. I had just had 2 heart attacks and had a couple of stints placed in my heart a couple of days prior. It took me a few weeks to get my mental capacity back after the medication they gave me. I thought that the dealer told me that I would need to get an emissions test. I thought I was to take the receipt from the emissions test and a form that the dealer gave me to the Motor Vehicles department. I did the emissions test (I later found that it had already been done) and I took the receipt and the form the dealer gave me to the department of motor vehicles. They didn't know why I was there. Evidently, the dealer had done all that for me and the DMV did not have record of it yet. What the dealer did not do, was replace the temporary license sticker that should have been in my back window. I was exhausted from all this running around in a strange city. I went back to Jason's apartment to wait for Jason to get home from work. We needed to get his insurance and I wanted to leave the next day. I parked Jason's car right outside his apartment, in his assigned spot. When Jason got home we found a nasty note on Jason's car. It said, "This is an unlicensed vehicle! If it is not moved within 30 min. the police will be called and the car towed." I realized that I should have informed the manager immediately when I parked the car there, but frankly I was too exhausted to climb the stars to their apartment. I now had to do that immediately. I knocked on their door and told them that I had just bought that car for Jason. I was so sorry that I had not told them immediately." Well "brother manager" met me with all the hostility of a raging bull. "Sister Manager" was right behind him getting her licks in too. His arms were flailing and he was screaming at me nose to nose "that there was no reason to yell about it" and saying something about the car being stolen. I said, really calmly, "no, you are absolutely right, there is no reason for anybody to get upset or to yell, the car is not stolen, I just bought it from a reputable dealer. I don't know the laws in Oregon. Apparently you do, I am simply asking for your help. Can you tell me what I need to do? I just bought the car and I am waiting for the license to come in the mail." Now he is starting to calm down. He told me, just as I suspected that it should have a sticker in the back window. I noticed some tape in the back window, so it must have come off at some point. I told him that I would call the dealer right away". I thanked him for his help, and I asked if it was parked in Jason's correct spot. He said it was. As we walked away Jason said, "Mom, I can't believe how you let him walk all over you!" I said, "Jason, did you get what you wanted?" "Yes." "Is your car getting towed away?" "No." "Does your manager look like an out of control idiot?" "Yes." "So, tell me again, who won?" "Well, yeah, but he just walked all over you." "No, I used my brain, and I walked all over him!"

We went to an independent dealer and got Jason's insurance. It was really expensive because he had never had insurance before. I told him, that at some point, he would find that if he totaled his car they would give him less for it than he would pay in insurance. At that point, he should drop that portion of his insurance. Now that he had a car he started doing odd construction jobs. While I was in Portland I also bought him a set of tools to make that easier for him and a computer to help him get his GED. He learned a lot and made lots of contacts doing this. The problem was that the jobs were short lived and he was always looking for his next job and he had no health insurance or sick leave. A few months after Jenny left, he was lucky enough to be home when he got a call from the carpenters union. They needed an apprentice carpenter to start immediately. Wow, this was the break he had been waiting for! He attended school at a local community college and soon he had his GED. For the next 3 or 4 years he drove his little car and went to all the classes that the carpenters union offered. He was working towards his Journeyman's level. He also became very active in his union. He had one set back during this time. He always walks if possible, especially if he is drinking. He was walking home from down town at night and he stepped in a hole in the sidewalk and broke his foot. He continued to walk another mile or so on his broken foot and the next day there was no way he could work. He was off for an extended period of time with a broken foot. He did not tell me nor communicate with me during this time. I found out because during this time he moved in the middle of the night and left a lot of junk in his apartment. I had given the brother and sister managing team my phone number and told them to call me if they ever had any problems with Jason or Jenny. Apparently when Jason was late paying his rent they did not consider that an emergency. Instead of calling me, they used this as an opportunity to evict him after 4 years of on time rent payments. They called me to report him "missing".

I tried to call him and the phone was disconnected, he didn't answer his cell phone. Now, I was worried. I called his union and said he was "missing", that I was worried and looking for him. The lady there told me, "No, he has a broken foot, but he is not missing I see him everyday." Now it was all becoming clear. He had found another apartment and left before they had the opportunity to evict him. He figured that I had paid the last months rent and that is the only way he would get use of that money is to use it up. As for damage deposit, there is no way he would ever get that back, it was difficult to move and clean with a broken foot so he would just get his money's worth there too by leaving all the stuff he didn't want. Need I say he left no forwarding address? The brother/sister management team called me on the pretense of wanting to know what to do with his belongings. I told them to sell it for the money owed. They said there is nothing worth selling. I told them to throw it away then. They complained that the apartment was really filthy. I really did not feel that it was my problem. What they really wanted was for me to drive to Portland and clean up his apartment. Would he then get his damage deposit back? I think not. They told me once that the sister really cleans the apartments exceptionally well and that she gets the damage deposits.

The second year of insurance came due on Jason's car insurance. I paid it as a birthday present. I told him that this was absolutely the last year that I would pay it. It would be cheaper for the third year. He had had no tickets or accidents. Still he was so shocked at the price that he remembered our discussion on dropping the comprehensive and that is what he did. Shortly after that, he skidded on some ice, hit a concrete barrier and totaled his car. He was somehow surprised that he had no insurance coverage. He called me, needing a car immediately. He really hated missing work. He was just recovering financially from being off with a broken foot. I reminded him of our discussion about dropping the comprehensive and told him that he had done the right thing. He was doing some private contracting at this time and really needed a truck. I went online and shopped the Portland area auto market. He missed the years where a teenager learns from his parents how to handle these things. He was 30 years old now but as innocent and as naïve as a 16 year old. Fortunately, he had a friend who was willing to take him to this dealer and help out. I was not willing to put anymore than $1000 down for him. I put $2000 down. I thought he had *no* credit. He had *bad* credit. It was utility companies, when he perceived a wrong that they perpetrated upon him, he refused to pay them. He felt victimized frequently. Now he was going to have to have a bigger down payment and a sky high interest rate. I established a really good relationship with the dealer. I asked him to really impress upon Jason why he has to pay this interest rate and to show him what his payments would have been if he had excellent credit. It was a very substantial difference. His friend was shocked too. I hope that he paid it for a year and then refinanced it. I don't know if he did because of his distrust of banks and finance companies. No, I don't know if he did it because of his general paranoia. I told him not to dare let a payment be late or let his insurance laps. I expected him to manage this himself. I told him I did not anticipate that he would need help, but as a last resort call me rather than default or be late. To work, he needs his truck and his loan requires that he carries insurance. He is paying a high price for having bad credit but he can build his credit by carrying this contract perfectly.

Now Jason is a journeyman. I know from my contact at his union hall that he is a key union member and is always working. He is a very good worker and very respected by his peers. He is known to be "very independent" but he is a good enough worker that apparently employers will put up with that. He is an active volunteer in a charity that repairs and fixes up senior citizens homes in the area. In fact, he is the contact person for that charity. My only picture of him in the last 10 years comes from a story on that project on his union's web site. He has recently moved again and is living with a room mate. This time it is male roommate. He claims that women are nothing but trouble and now avoids relationships with them. He still dates women but refuses or professes to refuse to let them live with him. The last time I talked to him was over a year ago. At that time, he was being sent by his union to El Salvador to monitor their national elections and protect the voters from intimidation at the polls. He was also going to meet with some medical personnel who wanted to unionize. We have traveled extensively in central and South American countries. We find it prudent to keep a low profile and not meddle in their politics. I warned him of how people disappear down there if they anger the wrong person. Knowing Jason, this would probably be an issue. It was very important that he understand this but I doubted that he heard me. I talked to him again when he returned and he repeated my speech to me like he was giving me a new revelation. I think it was a really good trip for him. He made some good friends and came home with a fresh look at life and at the United States. He stayed with some natives there and the food they served him was really meager. One day a fireman that was in the group with him said, "Come on Jason lets go get some real food." They did and Jason got very very sick. That surprised me because Jason broke all the food safety rules while growing up and traveling with us to Mexico and *never* got sick. I thought he was surely immune.

It has been Jason's habit to only call us when he is in pain or needs a rescue. He has dropped out of site for long periods of time, yet becomes offended when he isn't told immediately when some family issue comes up. It has been a really long time since he remembered us with a birthday card, Mother's day, Father's day or Christmas card. Yet, we don't think he is angry at us. My goal as his mother was to prepare him to take care of himself, knowing that I wouldn't always be here for him. I feel comfort in taking this non-communication to mean that my goal was achieved, though it does sadden me. I used to tense up whenever the phone would ring. I was always waiting for the other shoe to drop or the next emergency to occur. That is starting to go away now. After years and years of conditioning, I thought it never would. I no longer feel anger towards Phil for being so in denial and so at odds with me in the rearing of our kids. He would just go to bed when things would get in an upheaval. I would then be left to deal with it by myself. Those feelings sometimes resurface when our grandkids occasionally get rambunctious and he retreats to his bedroom. Now I send the kids in for stories. I never got over being angry about this but at the same time I would be glad that he was out of the picture because he was rarely of any help but more often a hindrance. He no longer feels anger towards me for leaving him out of the loop on our child rearing decisions and for carrying out my decisions regardless of his opinion. He was not sure enough of himself to really try to interfere. I was grateful for that. Deep down he knew that he was in denial. He did not want to be responsible for what might occur if he stopped me. Just before Jason was taken to Utah, I feared for our lives. I didn't know this kid anymore. He was violent and unpredictable.

It is really unusual for couples who have dealt with this kind of ordeal to stay together. When couples have such differing philosophies it is even more unusual that they remain in the marriage. The only way I can explain our perseverance is to say that, perhaps, I just took over and did what I felt needed to be done. Phil may have objected but I just continued and he was not forceful enough or sure of himself enough to interfere. We did argue at times, but Phil had such a poor parental role model that he must have realized that he needed to step back occasionally. There was never any question that he cared deeply. We had a wonderful marriage before we had our family and now we are having a wonderful marriage after. We are truly soul mates and best friends. It would have been such a tragedy had we not stayed together. I am so glad we did. There were times that we both wanted to run away and leave the other with all these problems. There was a time that I was making plans to take Brandi and leave Phil with Jason. At the time, I believed that Phil had already ruined Jason with his parenting or lack of it. Phil wanted to leave me with both kids and just run to Mexico. I would dream every night that I had a secret ability to just give a little push off and I could float above the earth. It was so pleasant. When I would reveal this ability in my dream, people were so amazed. I recently told Phil of this reoccurring dream I had had during that time. I was surprised to learn that he had that dream also. I now I feel that this was our bodies' way of giving us symbolic relief by allowing us to rise above our problems if only for a few minutes. Life is really good now. We have both retired and moved out of the dark and dreary Seattle and into a resort community called Saddlebrooke north of Tucson and south of Phoenix, Arizona.

15

Current state of affairs

Jason is a journeyman carpenter still living in Portland. He is active in his union and the secretary there tells me he is an important member of the union, he is well respected by the contractors and always has a job. I often visit the Portland carpenters union web site in an effort to have some knowledge of our son. I found his picture and an article about the charitable work he was involved in to help low income senior citizens. I got his number from the web site and we have tried to call him but he never returns our calls. Years of living on the street has stolen any feelings of family ties from him. I wonder often if he has any memories of the good times we had as a family. I recently had some really old 8 mm reel type home movies put on DVDs and sent him a copy. My worries for him center on loneliness, drugs, alcohol, job site injuries and disease due to his old lifestyle. My hope for him is that he is happy, healthy, fulfilled and feels he has no need for us anymore and therefore doesn't bother with contacting us. When he was on the street he only contacted us when he had a need or was hurting and this became a habit for him. I am sad that he doesn't want a relationship with us but that was a calculated risk, when I sent him to Utah. My constant goal for him was for him to be independent and self sustaining and a contributing member of the community. I believe he has reached that goal.

For some strange reason, he always gives our address on any loan or utilities applications. We often get calls from creditors when he defaults on something. In an effort to protect his privacy he is unwittingly giving us a lot of information about his continuing mismanagement of money. He still doesn't seem to know how life works. When he gets mad at a utility company or a store he refuses to pay what he owes them. He is totally messing up his credit this way. We just got another call for him from a probable creditor. I guess he still doesn't get it.

We miss him and think about him every day. Perhaps someday we can once again have a relationship with him but it is his choice. If he wants to drop out of our lives, that is his right.

Our daughter is now divorced and living in San Diego. She has her master's degree and a great job that she is very dedicated to. Brandi is a loving mother of two beautiful and adorable children and has a really good relationship with their father. Moving closer to our grandkids was a consideration at retirement. Our grandkids are a real joy in our lives. We take them on vacations and they come to visit us often. We indulge their passions. Horses are Cayla's love, so we always take her riding. We will send her to a horse camp when she is old enough. Billy loves snakes, fishing, dolphins and surfing. We call Billy "Mr. Science". Both kids are very intelligent and remember everything we teach or show them. Brandi says that after visiting with us, Billy will suddenly just explode with information on something fascinating or amazing that we told him. She has learned to no longer contradict him before calling me after she told him that there was no such thing as pink dolphins in the Amazon. He said, "Yes there is, Nana and Papa saw them!" Then he went on to explain why they are in fresh water and what makes them pink. I told Cayla that more than one cactus is called cacti and a baby cactus is called a pup. When we drove together back to San Diego she talked about all the cacti pups she saw all the way to San Diego.

We recently took them to Maui and provided Billy with surfing lessons. He was a natural. We followed up with more surfing lessons in San Diego. We will send him to surfing camp when he is old enough and willing to stay overnight without a parent or grandparent. Last Christmas we went on a one week cruise to Mexico. This summer we are going on a one week Alaska cruise. Next year we will take them to Grand Cayman Island for one week. We love backpack/adventure travel. Where we have a very loose itinerary and reserve only our airline round trip ticket and our first night hotel room. From there we strike out on our own and if we like a place we stay for a few days and if we don't we move on. We have set that type of travel aside for now because it is not something we would feel comfortable doing with kids. We really have only a few short years that the grandkids are going to want to go with us. For now, with the grandkids, resorts and cruises are perfect but when we no longer have them with us we will probably never go to another resort or on another cruise again.

We worry a little bit about our granddaughter, Cayla, because she has many traits that Jason had at the same age. She is responding well to discipline and is getting better. Fortunately, both of her parent's present a united front. Hopefully, we will be able to prevent the catastrophic events that Jason went through with our previous experience. That is why I am writing this book. It is an exercise in examining the events, analyzing the problem, and evaluating the solution.

Hopefully this will help or at least encourage or empower other parents with a similar child.

16

Hind Sight is 20/20—My Regrets

What would I do differently if I suddenly found myself with another child like Jason to raise?

First I would find a child psychologist. I would probably do this at about age 3 in Jason's case. I would expect to go through a few before I found one that I liked. When I first took Jason to a therapist it was for practical solutions to parenting problems. I did get that from some better than others. Later, as his problems progressed, I sought emotional help in dealing with an out of control child as well as practical solutions. After his problems worsened to the point of our feeling unsafe, I sought solutions by removing him from our home and placing him in a place where he could gain more education and we all could live in safety. When I did find a therapist that I wanted to stay with I would get the name of a pediatrician who would take a more serious interest in my child and his problems. One who was more willing to give referrals and to work with me aggressively.

I know it is difficult to get into the Behavioral Science Unit at Children's Hospital. Probably it is just as difficult to get into a similar facility in other states. However, we would definitely talk about that and I would request extensive testing for my child very early at Children's Hospital or at another similar facility. Unfortunately neurological testing was not done on Jason until he was a teenager.

If we found a learning difference, I would start discussing it with my child repeatedly until he understood that he had a learning difference *not* a disability BEFORE he noticed it through difficulty at school and his self-esteem was damaged. Then it would be simply be a fact of life—not a big embarrassment for him. He could then learn to deal with it. For example, Jason is a visual learner. I would teach him that he understands best by looking at a picture or writing a note to himself. That would be an easy concept for me to show him because I too am a visual learner and knowing that is a real help to me. I just carry a pad and pencil

90

when listening to complicated instructions and take notes or draw a quick sketch as I am being instructed.

I would keep a copy of his neurological tests handy. I would make copies for his file at school. I would refer to his testing results often when speaking to academic people. I would also give a copy to the district psychologist. I would paper the school district with these copies. I would request an IPP (Individual progress plan) and take a copy of his tests to this meeting and then monitor his progress. I would continually stress his learning style. I would take a copy of his tests to his teacher every year and periodically have him re-tested. I would speak to his teacher frequently. I would continually focus on his learning style. You really have to advocate for your child.

I would hire a tutor at early grade school and have that person work with the district psychologist and his teachers to boost his learning. I would hire a tutor because I know, for Jason; he would require an outsider to control him in a home tutoring situation. I was never able to do that for Jason. I believe this is typical of this type of child, not a shortcoming on my part. Again I would provide a copy of his neurological tests to the tutor. Remember, that while there are really caring professionals in the schools, ultimately YOU are the one that has ONLY your child's best interest at heart. **ALWAYS ADVOCATE FOR YOUR CHILD.** It really angers me that Jason went without anyone suggesting neurological testing until he was a teenager! I am not a professional! I did not know that there existed such a thing, but I did know that something was wrong and I was constantly asking for help and advice.

I would introduce and re-introduce family counseling frequently on an as needed basis. I would go on-line to the Tough Love website and if you don't have a group in your area; I would start one. You really need the peer support. You will be amazed how many wonderful, concerned, intelligent parents are in your community with the very same problems.

If he still got out of control I would send him to the school in Utah or a similar school at a much younger age. He really needed to be in a more controlled environment at a much younger age. What he needed would be impossible to provide in a private home in a private neighborhood.

I would start random drug testing at about 6th grade. It would be a fact of life in our home. I would also do it with our daughter, lest one slip through the cracks. This would be accompanied with a talk about the importance of staying drug free. I regret not recognizing his drug use earlier and not coming down on him like World War III. I regret not realizing that when your child is using, you are no longer talking to your child, you are talking to the drug. That is why reason does not work! Eventually we did random drug tests through our doctor with our child's consent. This was a necessary requirement due to privacy laws for our doctor; it would not be a requirement in your home. You can now buy over the counter drug tests. When I was dealing with this I had to run the sample to my doctor's office and wait for results. I regret not doing it sooner and then sending him to a treatment program immediately on a positive test. I noticed that there is now a drug test in the drug store that costs about $30 and it tests for Metha-amphetamine, ecstasy, cocaine, marijuana and a number of drugs. It is my guess that you can use it for multiple tests. Today that would become a staple in our house and surprise tests would be frequent. Before the age of 12 you can commit your child against their wishes—I think 12 was one year to soon for Jason, but the younger a child is, the easier it is to manipulate him into committing himself.

I would be much less generous with material things and I would not be so permissive. Jason really needed structure. I regret that in an effort to make my children's childhood easier and more pleasant, I was way too permissive. I wanted my children to have an easier and happier life than Phil and I had. Our parents were so very strict. I should have said "no" to more activities and talked to other parents more. I should have demanded retribution from him for the terrible disrespect he showed us and the terrible language he used. If I had it to do over, his room would have only a mattress and blanket. I would provide one change of clothes daily of my choosing. There would be no all black with spikes and offensive pictures on the shirts. The situation would remain this way until his behavior changed.

I regret ever having alcohol in the house. It was a poor example, used for self medication to help me cope with the chaos Jason created. Although, when I recognized the problem I corrected it immediately.

I regret letting him see me get angry at his father over his interference with my discipline (i.e. "what are you doing to him now, Cindy!"). The knowledge that it made me furious only encouraged Jason to get us fighting. Our anger at each other took the focus off Jason and off his misbehavior and made him feel powerful.

I regret that I was such a slow learner in learning to stay calm, soft spoken and logical when Jason was pushing my buttons and trying to incite a riot. *When you loose your composure you give up your power*. At that point Phil would usually jump in and further anger me. Jason would actually grin at this redirection of attention. I would just go crazy. This is a skill that all parents should develop far before the birth of their first child. It is really critical especially when you have an oppositional child. It also is a great tool in dealing with my very nasty sister's attacks.

I regret that Jason proclaims to be an atheist and I believe it is mostly my fault. When Jason was in later grade school, I sent him to a Christian summer camp. He came home all motivated and full of Christian teaching. One day he said, "Where could all this have come from if God didn't make It" and started naming space and trees and animals and so on. I said, "Just because you don't know, doesn't mean it was made by a God." My point, was to teach him to *think* not to just assign the unknown to a supernatural answer for everything that you don't understand like they did in the dark ages. I am profoundly sorry for that conversation because nothing I have said afterwards could undo it.

I regret not removing his door and everything he owned from his room, while he was on run away status, instead of cleaning and organizing it. His room should have been bare and door less 99% of the time because of his behavior. He did not deserve all that he had with that attitude. That was so effective that I would gladly rent a POD and store his belongings locked up on our property. If he went crazy and tried to break into it I would just pick up the telephone and have them come and pick it up the POD and keep it in their warehouse. I regret not teaching my kids to be more respectful of authority and rules.

I would make myself very familiar with the juvenile code for my state. For example, Washington now allows a parent to go before a judge with their child and set up behavior expectations. Failure for the child to comply with these expectations puts the child in contempt of court. I would learn about this early so that you have another weapon in your arsenal just in case. This is a fairly new law for Washington and it did not exist when I needed it. I really regret that the current Washington juvenile code came too late for us. I know that several tragedies contributed to by the former juvenile code forced our legislatures to make some changes. If I were doing this over now I would get a family law attorney to guide me through all the laws that I now have available to me. I would go before a judge and ask that Jason be required to not run away, maintain a curfew, go to school, take random drug tests and stay off drugs and alcohol, not steal or break any other laws. He would be in contempt of court if he failed to follow these requirements and he would be sent into juvenile detention. He really hated juvenile detention. I avoided it for too long, thinking that he would be exposed to really bad kids. The fact is that once he starts using drugs he IS one of the really bad kids. If he hasn't lost his morals yet he soon will. Once again, you are not dealing with your child now; you are dealing with the drug.

Those are my regrets and hind sights. My wish for my readers is that they have fewer regrets than I and that this book helps them to avoid some of them. Above all else, stay strong.

17

The Factors That Got Him off the Street and off Drugs

I am often asked what I feel turned him around. First of all I know that he was very intimidated by older street people. They were mean and very intimidating to him. He avoided all shelters and services where he might encounter them. At the same time he was getting too old to access services provided to young street people. The familiar doors that previously enabled him were now closing to him and the new doors opening were not appealing. He was also maturing. I don't believe that a drug user matures at the same rate as a non-drug user does. It appears that their emotional growth stops or severely slows at the age they start using, but he was maturing slowly. His brain was reaching full growth. He now has the ability to see how his behavior today might affect the future for him. It was not a pretty picture. The homeless kids out there on the street were now looking pretty silly and they were intimidated by *him*. He now had a girl friend that had been on the street as long as he had been and was exactly the same age. She was maturing also. They were both getting tired of the street. We were always afraid of him getting trapped in the backwaters and not being able to escape. That is why we were always willing to attempt to give him a hand up—not a hand out, when he claimed to want to get off the street. We were becoming very careful. We had had several failed rescue attempts due to his manipulation and lack of commitment. We were becoming harder to manipulate by his view, unwilling to be manipulated by our own view. We were tightening the screws. However we realized, he was damaged goods and he really needed help. Also, we had to constantly remind ourselves that an addict was a master manipulator. It was a very difficult and delicate balancing act.

I also believe he had made lots of enemies out on the street. Former friends that he had double crossed or racist skin heads that would recognize him as the enemy. There were probably drug dealers that he owed money to as well. Also, he felt that he was well known by the local police and not popular with them. I think he felt it was just time to rejoin the real world.

He was on the street and probably out of state when he kicked. At any rate, I was not with him when he kicked any of his addictions so I can't speak to that. What I can say is that Jason is the most stubborn and the most determined person I have ever met and if he wanted to kick he would kick or he would die trying.

Postscript: I am most pleased to report that Jason has once again surfaced, at age 36. This is the update that I feel compelled to report.

My father had a stroke on New Years day 2007. At first he appeared to be getting better but then he started to decline rapidly. He had always said that he would really like to see Jason again before he died. They had been so close when Jason was growing up. Desperate to make that happen I wrote a simple letter to Jason, in care of his union, saying that his Grandfather was very ill and that his dying wish was to see him again. I gave the address of the home he was in and a list of phone numbers, ours included. A couple of weeks later Jason called me. He said he was not angry at anybody, he just didn't realize it had been years since we talked. He gave me his current address and phone number. He told me that he made his journeyman level but that he is now working for the union, as an organizer, covering a four state area and he is rarely home. He called as soon as he got my letter and he promised to go see his grandfather in the next couple of weeks. My father died one week later, never having seen Jason again. I called Jason to inform him, he was very upset that he didn't get there in time. I reminded him that his grandmother was still alive and I warned him not to be *too late* again. Although he goes to Seattle frequently, he still has not visited her.

During one of our recent phone conversations, I ask Jason if Metha-amphetamine was his drug of choice, as I suspected. He said no, that he didn't use meth for very long at all. I know he used it while he was still living with us because it made him so very violent. He said that after he was on the street he turned to heroin. I reminded him that he told me that once but that I didn't believe him because he went to jail shortly after that and he didn't go through withdrawal. He said that he tried to kick it several times before he was actually successful and that might have been during a short time that he was clean. I am so glad I didn't believe the heroin story at the time—I don't think that I could have handled that knowledge emotionally. Although I know now that meth is every bit as dangerous as heroin and harder to kick. Jason is still drug free but he says he thinks about drugs every day. I worried out loud that he may someday slip back into using. He said, "Oh, no, I've learned my lesson."

During that same phone call he said, "Mom, I don't want to make you mad, but all those schools and hospitals you sent me to and all those psychologists and therapists were worthless. I just twisted them around and manipulated them to get what I wanted and now I am so far left that I am way further left than democrat. He just can't seem to hide his oppositional/defiant personality. He knows that I am very much a conservative, politically. I believe that he assumed that his therapists were conservative also because they talked about choices and logical consequences and taking responsibility-just like we do. I also believe that those are all important qualities of a conservative. However, I am rather surprised that he understands that. What he doesn't understand is that at some point the therapists and psychologists became my lifeline and the schools and hospitals just served to contain him long enough to educate him. He gets really passionate when speaking about his far left politics and has all kinds of pseudo facts to back up his points. I believe that radical liberals have their place in society-however angry they make me. It is part of our check and balance system and the freedom of speech that we hold so dear. It is best that we avoid political discussions with Jason. No one's mind is ever going to change. Contrary to my conservative politics, I am not blind to history. Therefore, I do believe in the value of unions and I am proud that he has found his place in the world.

Jason goes to Las Vegas often because his union has a training center there. He commented on how some of his colleagues go out on the strip and party and gamble into the night. He says that he does not like to gamble and he is not going to sit in class the next day hung-over. Also, he recognizes that that kind of behavior doesn't look good to your boss. I guess he did pick up some work ethic along the way. Who would have ever thought that someday Jason would have a job that he is absolutely devoted to, that he would have an expense account, a union provided car and charge card, be flying first class and staying in Hilton hotels while making a great salary and really loving it. He says "I love this job; I get to do what I enjoy most, manipulate people, piss them off, and cause trouble, what a great job! He really does care about the union workers though and has real empathy for men trying to support their families. Non union shops will often fire people who are trying to unionize. Jason warns them that this will happen up front and when it does happen Jason makes it his most urgent priority to get these people into better paying union jobs right away. Surprisingly, the union's building contractors really respect him. The secretary at the union told me that Jason is one of their most skilled and dependable workers and is always sought after by their contractors. Of course, he is rarely working as a carpenter these days. He is working full time for the union.

One of the tactics that the union uses to fight against non union employers is to gather personal information on their CEOs—like how many kids they have, their names and ages, where they live, what their activities are, how much their bonuses and their salaries are. Sometimes they are followed. This is done mostly to intimidate them. Suddenly Jason noticed that he was being followed and watched. He started greeting these people in a friendly manner when he would see them until they finally got bored and left him alone. He says he knows that there are people who want to kill him, but the people that let him see them are not the ones to be afraid of. Intimidation is their game. If they wanted to harm him he would already be harmed.

Does this fact worry me as a mother? Not really. Jason is really smart, observant and street wise. I have always said that there are worse things than dying. I believe that Jason has experienced most of them. I believe that in my mind and in my heart I have experienced all of them. I feel content now and secure that I can finish out my life in peace.

The End

978-0-595-48862-9
0-595-48862-5

Printed in the United Kingdom by
Lightning Source UK Ltd., Milton Keynes
140011UK00001B/135/P

9 780595 488629